Losing Out

GE

Losing Out

Sexuality and adolescent girls

Sue Lees

Hutchinson

London   Melbourne   Sydney   Auckland   Johannesburg

Hutchinson Education Ltd

An imprint of Century Hutchinson Ltd
62–65 Chandos Place, London WC2N 4NW
and 51 Washington Street, Dover,
New Hampshire 03820, USA

Hutchinson Publishing Group (Australia) Pty Ltd
16–22 Church Street, Hawthorn, Melbourne,
Victoria 3122

Hutchinson Group (NZ) Ltd
32–34 View Road, PO Box 40–086, Glenfield,
Auckland 10

Hutchinson Group (SA) (Pty) Ltd
PO Box 337, Bergvlei 2012, South Africa

First published 1986

Set in Linotron Baskerville

Printed and bound in Great Britain by
Anchor Brendon Ltd, Tiptree, Essex

British Library Cataloguing in Publication Data
Lees, Sue
  Losing out : sexuality and adolescent
  girls.
  1. Adolescent girls—sexual behaviour
  I. Title
  306.7'0941   HQ27.5

Library of Congress Cataloging in Publication Data
Lees, Sue
  Losing out
  Includes Bibliographies and index.
  1.   Adolescent girls — England — London
  — Sexual Behavior.
  2.   Youth — England — London — Sexual Behavior
  — Moral and ethical aspects.   I.   Title.
  HQ27.5.L44   1986   306.7'088055   86–3137

ISBN 0 09 164101 2

Contents

Acknowledgements

This research has taken five years to complete. Celia Cowie and I conducted the interviews and group discussions, with the help of Linsey Buck. Celia was a full-time Research Fellow attached to the project and Linsey a full-time student on placement. All three of us had children under 10 and hardly a day passed without some crisis or other – usually involving children's illnesses – disrupting the smooth running of the research design. Ellen Graham transcribed many of the interviews with great accuracy and speed, funded by the Nuffield Foundation.

Unfortunately at this point everything came to a halt when I fell ill with an obscure virus called Guillam Barree which left me totally paralysed for three months and took me another six months to recover from. By this time, Celia was not in a position to be able to write up the research, and I have reluctantly done so on my own. I would like to emphasize, however, that Celia contributed to many of the ideas developed in this book, as well as to the actual fieldwork.

All in all, therefore, it is something of a miracle that this book was completed at all, and without the encouragement of many friends and my children it would not have been possible. I would like to thank in particular Celia, Linsey, Esther and Ellen, and also Claire L'Enfant, John Lea, Diana Leonard and Sue Sharpe. Last I would like to thank Susan Pritchard who typed the manuscript and all the girls who gave time and enthusiasm to the interviews and discussions.

To Dan and Jose.

Introduction

What is it like to be an adolescent girl in the 1980s? Is it very different from the 1950s? Has the re-emergence of the Women's Movement and greater awareness of sexual inequality, along with the impact of the pill, led to greater sexual freedom? Why is it that girls who at 15 are doing as well as if not better than boys at school and have high career aspirations do not fulfil them? How is life different for a girl than for a boy? Does friendship mean the same to girls as boys or is it true that girls are so bitchy that they can never be true friends? How do girls view boys and boyfriends? Do girls live in different social worlds to boys? Why are girls called 'slags' and frequently sexually abused?

In embarking on the research I wanted to throw light on the way girls are disadvantaged – not merely in terms of fewer career opportunities, greater domestic responsibilities and less freedom to pursue leisure activities, but in less tangible ways – by attempting to examine the way power relations between girls and boys constrict and limit girls' material experience. By asking girls to describe their experiences – what they talked about, how they had fun, how they saw boys and what was important in friendship – I hoped to explore the meanings and understandings by which girls live their lives. By eliciting *the terms* on which they describe and handle their world I hoped to discover the general principles by which girls can transform themselves from being victims to being in control of their lives. We[1]* initially asked girls about five main areas of their lives. However it gradually became clear how circumscribed girls' lives were by the mere fact of being girls; this led to a focus on how it is that sexuality impinged on their lives – not so much in terms of actual sexual experience but in their day-to-day social life where

* Superior figures refer to the Notes following each chapter.

their gender was a constant source of comment and often abuse. It became clear that, whatever their social class, girls are defined primarily by their sexual reputation – whether they are 'flighty', 'tartish', 'cheap' girls or whether they are 'nice', 'respectable', 'marriageable', 'one man' girls. The mere fact of being a girl affects everything she does. Girls are defined in terms of their sexuality and exist in a culture that is patriarchal, where women are subordinate to men and are seen first and foremost as wives, mistresses, mothers, spinsters, lesbians or whores.[2]

This study is based on research carried out in three London comprehensives in the early 1980s. It involved interviews or group discussions with about a hundred 15- to 16-year-old girls from varied social class and ethnic groups. The first two schools were mixed; both had women head teachers and were attempting to put into force an equal opportunities programme. One had a high proportion of black, Greek and Asian girls and the other a mainly white working-class intake – most of the children in both schools had been brought up in the area. After interviewing the head and obtaining permission from the ILEA to go into the schools, the form teachers in the fourth year were asked to suggest to the girls in their classes that they should form groups of friends if they were willing to take part in group discussions. The importance of allowing girls to select their own groups must be stressed. Girls are noted for forming into small groups that are often exclusive and even hostile to other girls. What can be said in a small group of friends would not be expressed more publicly. The size of the groups was never more than five or six. Apart from providing a rich source of material, as the discussions did seem to 'take off' when the girls lost their self-consciousness, the groups provided an essential warming-up period in which the girls were introduced to the research and the interviewer in a relaxed and informal way. The girls were then either interviewed on their own or, if they preferred, in the presence of a friend. This often seemed to make the girls feel more at ease. All the discussions and interviews were tape recorded and later transcribed. We chose to use non-directive, semi-structured interviews as they allow 'a comprehensive expression of the subject's feelings and beliefs and of the frame of reference within which feelings and beliefs take on personal significance' (Selltiz 1965).* This type of interview, as opposed to more formal quantifiable methods, enables the subjects' responses to be followed up, and allows them to be more specific and more revealing of both intimate material and the connections across material that indicate the social context of those feelings, beliefs and ideas.

A year later the research was repeated in a single sex comprehensive that had previously been direct grant and had the reputation of being 'middle-class'. Mainly middle-class girls from this school were interviewed in an attempt to throw light on the impact of class on the way girls describe their day-to-day experience. Some of the girls interviewed were also given a questionnaire to fill in about their home circumstances, parental occupations, education, religion, and interests, and about the girls' own friendship networks. We also invited some of the girls from two schools to video two days of group discussions at the polytechnic. This was later made into a short video film. Some of these discussions were also later transcribed. The video was shown to the girls and they were asked what they thought about it.

Very few comparable studies of girls are available, and researchers have commented on the inaccessibility of girls. These other studies were mainly carried out in youth clubs. By conducting interviews and discussions during school time rather than the girls' own time we avoided encroaching on their time and provided a welcome diversion from classes. They were not only willing to talk but prepared to discuss intimate questions about their lives with what appeared to be openness and frankness as well as verve and humour. This is not to say that the girls did not view us as different from themselves, and this might have affected their responses. Several commented on our clothes – wearing dungarees suggested to them that we were lesbian – and several were perplexed by our marital status or lack of it. One of us was living with her boyfriend and their child but had never been married and many of the girls found this extraordinary. It was clearly more acceptable to be separated with children than never to have married. It is impossible to know how far such factors influenced the course of the interviews. We usually tried

---

* Full references quoted in the text can be found in the Notes and references at the end of each chapter.

to avoid answering personal questions during the course of the interview but would say that when it was finished we would tell them anything about ourselves that they wanted to know. We thought that to divulge personal details during the interview might lead to biasing what the girls said – interviewees often want to please the interviewer and may say what they think she wants to hear. Since we were bringing up very personal issues it was particularly important that the girls should see us as accepting of any feelings they expressed. The fact that we elicited little or no discussions of sexual relations between girls should not be seen as a shortcoming of our research. As I have explained, our research did not begin as an explicit study of sexual relations but of the general terms in which girls described their lives. Our research method allowed the girls to speak for themselves and what emerged, as this book will show, was the power of patriarchal culture – exemplified by the slag/drag dichotomy – in constraining and determining the social existence of the girls, irrespective of their own sexual predilections. A lesbian girl would certainly be no less subject to these constraints than any other girl as in any case the patriarchal culture makes it very difficult for girls to give autonomous expression to their sexual desires.

We used unstructured interviews as a means of probing the meanings the girls attached to five aspects of their lives – school, friendship, boys, sexuality and their expectations for the future. It is more than a purely descriptive study. By focusing on *the terms* girls use to describe their lives rather than asking them structured questions, light was thrown on what their experiences – of school, boys, sex and so on – meant to them and how those individually experienced feelings are socially structured. It is important to understand that what the girls say cannot be taken as a simple reflection of reality. I was not interested in whether what the girls said was true or not but in the terms with which they described their experiences. I remember asking one girl whether there was anything really important about adolescent girls that she wanted people to know about and she replied 'That they're not all cheap.' This is how she imagined most people viewed adolescent girls 'when you go into a pub or somewhere y'know nudge, nudge, nudge, "She's a bit of alright" they say'. To understand why this girl wanted people to know that she and other girls like her were not cheap involves realizing how con-

stricted girls' lives are by the unfair relations between the sexes
and the whole structure of sex–gender relations. What the girls
say has a shared though hidden organization that structures the
way they relate to the world.

The main aim of the research is to raise questions about the
way individual experience is socially constructed – and, in particular, since it is so crucial to a girl's identity, sexual experience.
Generalizations about patriarchal power and the control by men
of women's sexuality and labour are frequently cited in the
feminist literature but little attempt has been made to describe
how power is exercised in the sexual domain and to examine the
mechanisms – both material and ideological – that underlie this
dominance. How sexuality is talked about, thought about, dis-
played and structured is a crucial aspect of social life. The
underlying premise of this approach is that there is more than
one root – that anatomy is destiny – of women's subordination.
The idea that sexuality is socially constructed implies that our
individual experience is a product of ideologies, social practices
and social structures. This research is an attempt to focus on the
way sex, race and class are experienced in the day-to-day life of
adolescent girls. Though the mere fact of being a girl seems to a
great extent to determine the way girls experience life, their
class and race also contribute to their social subordination. This
is reflected in such terms of abuse as 'black cunt' and 'dirty
(implying lower-class) whore'. These terms combine class, race
and sex abuse.

There are perhaps three main reasons why sexual relations
have been neglected in studies of adolescents. First, youth culture studies have focused on boys to the exclusion of girls and
sex–gender relations. Not only have these studies failed to discuss the savage chauvinism of male youth culture but often the
descriptions of rock bands, skinheads and the cattle market
atmosphere of the local dance hall have embraced a 'celebration
of masculinity'. These studies have not merely accepted sexism
uncritically, they have often, through depicting them romanti-
cally, extolled sexism. Second, I shall argue, the day-to-day experience of sexism to which girls are subject is rarely mentioned
or examined because it is accepted as an inevitable part of life –
due to the common-sense understanding of sexuality as 'natural'
and biological and therefore unchangeable. This transforms the

experience of very unfair relations between the sexes into an acceptance of those relations as natural. Third, when sexuality has been studied – mainly by psychologists or sexologists – focus has been on the sexual act (male penetration of the female) out of the context of social relationships and ignoring the power relations involved.

The neglect of girls in studies of youth

Research on adolescents is almost exclusively about boys – or youth as they are commonly described. When girls do make an appearance in studies of youth culture they are usually seen in ways that are marginal, or which uncritically reinforce a stereotyped image of women. Discussions about them are often in the context of sex with such comments as 'obviously the boys are interested in girls – they clearly talk about girls and sex a good deal of the time they are together' (Whyte 1943). This equating of girls with sex is a reflection of the way that women and girls are commonly represented in terms of their sexuality rather than as human beings.

The words woman and girl are intrinsically bound up with feminine and frequently sexual categories. Two researchers who studied a mixed group of boys and girls in the north-east noticed that this way of categorizing girls often rendered them invisible. Even before marriage lads avoided referring to their girlfriends by name – 'me lass' was far more common. This became even more pronounced on marriage. One young man who was particularly well known to them only divulged his wife's name after nine months. The researchers concluded that 'this depersonalization reflects a process which is nation-wide: women, not referred to in their own right, are made peripheral and so become invisible to the mind' (Marshall and Berrill 1984).

This may be one reason why sociologists have failed to notice girls. In discussing the absence of girls from the study of education Sandra Acker commented:

A Martian who attempted to find out about British education would conclude that numerous boys but few girls go to secondary modern schools, that there are no girls public schools, that there are almost no influential adult women of any sort, that ... women rarely make the ritual transition called from school to work and never go to colleges for further education (Acker 1981).

This may also explain why teachers find it more difficult to learn girls' names than boys' and why boys receive a disproportionate share of teachers' time, as has been shown in a number of studies of classroom interaction. Even when teachers try to give girls more attention they find it difficult to give them as much attention as they give to boys. Another common practice is to categorize grown women as 'girls'. Women in prison are invariably called 'girls' and even women delegates at the 1983 Labour Party Conference were annoyed at the party's chairman, Mr Sam McCluskie, referring to them as girls. When Lesley Courcouf from Hackney Labour Party launched her appeal against this she made it to 'Comrade Chairboy and the boys'.

Defining girls in terms of their sexuality rather than their attributes and potentialities is a crucial mechanism in ensuring their subordination to boys and men. It means that girls live in a very different social world to boys – one where being a girl determines everything they do. Girls are depicted as nude pin-ups in the gutter press, as sex objects in adverts, as appendages of men, as objects of male lust or as victims of male violence. Girls and women are rarely depicted as workers although 9 million women work – 40 per cent of the work force. Women's contributions to production and their role in society are rarely recognized. Marion Scott points out that in third world countries women play a crucial role in farming but this is certainly not the impression you would get from geography books (Scott 1980). Even women who have achieved positions of authority – and few do – are often described in press reports in terms of their appearance or dress, rather than their interests, opinions or personality.

Few studies of adolescent girls exist and little is known about how girls experience life in what is often depicted as the turbulent period of adolescence. Myths abound – about the increase in adolescent promiscuity heralded by the availability of the pill and greater freedom, the problem of teenage pregnancy and girls who are 'beyond control' of their parents. Boys, on the other hand, have been the subject of numerous studies. The study of youth culture, which of course means male youth culture, developed in the 1960s and 1970s into a subject area of its own within sociology. Gender relations were scarcely mentioned and the subordination of girls to boys was taken for granted rather than analysed. For example, Fyvel refers in his study of Teddy Boys to 'dumb passive, teenage girls crudely painted' (Fyvel 1963) and girls flit in and out of the pages as sex objects in the boys' eyes. In response to criticism about the exclusion of girls from these studies it was claimed that, due to the paucity of female researchers and the absurd assumption that therefore gender could not be studied, male sociologists could find no-one to write about girls. Others said that they could find no girls to write about – girls were not on the street, participated little in drug taking, delinquency, sport or other areas of concern to male sociologists – dancing, for example, although it is as popular as sport has been almost entirely neglected by sociologists. As Angela McRobbie commented 'Very little seems to have been written about the role of girls in youth cultural groupings in general; they are absent from the classic subcultural ethnographic studies: the "pop" histories, personal accounts, or journalistic surveys' (McRobbie and Garber 1975). Even if it is true that girls participate less in drug taking and delinquency, it is untrue that they are not involved in group activities or on the street. What is more likely is that girls have been overlooked. One sociologist even claimed that he could not discuss girls since he had not experienced female adolescence himself and went on to depict boys hanging around street corners on a Saturday night discussing 'footy' without a girl in sight. When I recently published an article that focused on girls I received several letters complaining that my study was biased and meaningless as I had failed to interview boys. One boy wrote it was 'totally biased towards the female point of view'. A study of girls is so unusual that it can be discarded as biased.

The construction of sexuality

This study is an attempt to explore the way girls describe their experience in order to throw light on the way individual experience is socially constructed. This is a concept which is extremely difficult to grasp. We all experience life as individuals – we feel, think, make and fall out with friends, perhaps fall in love, make plans and so on – which makes it hard to appreciate the way in which many of our experiences are caught up with ideas and definitions of femininity and masculinity and are constrained by these social definitions. It is only by comparing how different girls describe their experiences that it becomes clear that masculine and feminine behaviour is subject to different social rules and operates within different norms. It is not just that some behaviour is considered appropriate for a boy and not for a girl – for example swearing usually enhances a boy's position with his class-mates but a girl is likely to be regarded as 'unfeminine' and lower class. More important than these social expectations is the way that norms operate to limit girls' and boys' experience where the assumption is that certain behaviour is 'natural' for a boy but not for a girl and vice versa. The idea that experiences are socially structured conflicts with the common-sense assumption that our behaviour is either a matter of free choice or is natural and biologically given. The way free choice is socially constrained is rarely discussed and differences between the way girls and boys are expected to behave and experience life is attributed to biological differences.

Much of the confused thinking about sexuality and the failure to acknowledge the way conceptions of masculinity and femininity are socially rather than biologically constructed stems from essentialist ideas about some behaviour being 'natural' and therefore unalterable. It is regarded as natural for girls to be attracted to boys, unnatural for girls to have intense relationships with the same sex; natural for them to enjoy domesticity and to want to get married and have children, but unnatural to want a career that would conflict with marriage or to put their main energies into sport or creative activities. Most of all a girl is expected to put others before herself and to be caring and unselfish. Sexuality is looked on as the epitome of natural behaviour. It is natural for men to be promiscuous but unnatural for women to be so, natural for the woman to try and 'catch' a man and entice him into marriage, unnatural for a woman to live without a man.

These myths about the naturalness of masculine and feminine behaviour are very difficult to challenge because they are so embedded in common sense. I remember when my daughter was young her grandfather saw her playing with a brush and commented 'There you are, you can see how feminine and domesticated she is going to be when she grows up – a proper little woman.' The difficulty of challenging such assumptions is that evidence for naturalness is usually drawn from the observation that some behaviour is more typical of girls than boys. Even when this is the case – and often, as in this incident, it is due more to selective perception than to what actually occurred – and girls are found to be doing more housework and participating less in sport, this merely shows how effectively social norms work. What is suggested by the attribution of naturalness is that the behaviour is unchangeable and should be left untouched.

The intransigence of this belief that sex is natural and biological exists in the face of irrefutable historical and anthropological evidence that sex, far from being natural, is highly malleable. Sexual patterns of behaviour have varied remarkably at different historical periods; indeed they vary from culture to culture. Everyday concepts of male and female sexuality deny this evidence and still rest on the assumption that sexual behaviour is biological. This link perhaps emerges from the obvious association between sex and reproduction. Though the launching of the birth control pill meant that sex could potentially be separable from reproduction, the biological link between sex and reproduction has led to the belief that sexuality itself – sexual behaviour and sexual norms – is a product of biology rather than of culture. In this way male and female sexuality are conceptualized very differently and the difference is falsely attributed to biology. Male sexuality is seen as a force or natural energy that seeks release – it is heterosexual and involves a progression from arousal to penetration and orgastic release. It is a bit like a missile – once launched there is no stopping it – and the launching is the arousal phase. I remember my mum warning me not to excite a man lest he should be carried away and overcome with 'natural' passion – that if a man was aroused he could not 'stop' even if the woman was not willing. Harry O'Reilly, a retired New York police officer, comments wryly about this idea:

How can a man argue that a woman 'led him beyond his endurance'? Whoever heard of anyone dying of an erection? Men have been suppressing erections since time immemorial. ... The idea of the 'terminal erection' is a myth we have been perpetuating for years (O'Reilly 1984).

This argument is used as a defence in rape trials where, if a woman has given the impression that she is attracted to a man and he is aroused, then even if she backs away he can argue that he cannot stop. His sexuality is regarded as uncontrollable. Like-wise, an argument often heard in defence of prostitution is that it provides an outlet for male sexuality that if unreleased would lead to more rapes and assaults. The idea that men need sex in the same way that they need food is implicit in this idea. Women on the other hand do not only not need sex but are considered to be unnatural if they seek it – at least with someone other than a man that they love. Female sexuality is regarded as more passive and weaker than male sexuality and often associated with motherhood and reproduction. Promiscuous sex is re-garded as unnatural (or even subhuman); thus sex is seen in terms of its reproductive functioning, in terms of love for women and conquest for men, symbolized by a genital hetero-sexuality which men initiate and control. Men are involved in sexual acts and conquests; women are the objects of male desire.

What we need to understand is the way social practices and systems of representation operate and appear to work without any direct coercion. In order to grasp how the cultural codes of behaviour are understood and are effective at keeping women in their place we need to examine the terms on which girls enter into social life and the way those terms both limit and constrict their choices. The following piece, from the *News of the World*, illustrates how crossed communication and misunderstandings arise from the different codes of behaviour a boy and a girl are subject to:

A teenage girl gave 20 year old Anthony Davies two love bites during a disco necking session. And when he walked her home she suggested taking a short cut through a cemetery, a court heard.

'I knew it wasn't a short cut, so I thought I was on to a good thing', Davies told police later. But when they sat on a bench and he tried to have sex, the 17 year old girl pushed him away and said 'No stop it'. Davies indecently assaulted her and said he loved her. When the girl sat up to leave, he pushed her back on the bench and ripped her dress exposing her breast. 'He then punched her in the face, and as the girl screamed tore her pants off' said Mr Peter Rouch prosecuting at Carmarthen Crown Court. She managed to escape and as she ran away Davies shouted 'You'd better not tell anyone, because if you do I'll get you' (Dec. 1983).

This report illustrates the way that far from being a natural instinct, sexual activity is governed by norms and expectations which can result in the boy misinterpreting what the girl intends. The way a boy or girl experiences sexual desire is constrained by the assumptions that are made about the nature of female and male sexuality and by the different implications the expression of sexuality has for a girl and a boy. Sexual acts are negotiated within these forceful constraints. Here the boy thinks he is 'on to a good thing', that the girl is willing to have sex with him. It is after all 'natural' – or as I argue, socially expected – for a boy to be 'after one thing'. Having sex enhances a boy's masculinity and he could gain kudos from boasting to friends that he could persuade girls to go the whole way. This is not to deny that he clearly feels attracted and aroused by the girl. The girl too seems to have been sexually aroused – she gave him two love bites at the disco. But to her to have sex has different implications – not only would she risk pregnancy but her reputation, which rests not on conquests but on sexual abstinence, would be threatened. The boy implies he has been 'led on' and she provoked the attack that follows (by taking a short cut through the cemetery which he did not think was a short cut). The violence that follows is not acceptable within the norms of sexual morality but it is not surprising that lines get crossed and misunderstandings arise when the social pressures and personal outcome of a sexual encounter are so different for the boy and for the girl.

This hardly depicts a 'romantic' snapshot of adolescent sexual relations but it is by no means unusual. Sexual advance merging into violence is not totally unacceptable and is regarded by many as 'giving a girl what she really wants' or 'keeping a woman in her place'. It is an extension of the very unfair way sexual relations are structured. The boy's claim that he loved her as he indecently assaulted her is an indication of how confused 'sexual desire' and 'love' often become. It is love that legitimates a sexual relationship and the boy's declaration can be seen as either an attempt to imply that he is not just 'after one thing' or a ploy to reassure the girl. However his action clearly indicates that there is not much love in the encounter but desire merging into violence.

In a book on sex education in schools Carol Lee described how when she asked classes to role play a court case where a 15-year-old girl had been raped, the boy was never found guilty by a class *whatever the circumstances*. Assumptions were made that if the girl was coming home alone at 11 p.m. she must be a slut or that if she was not a virgin then that meant that 'she really wanted it'. Whenever rape was discussed there were at least a couple of boys who said: 'But women really want it, Miss', or 'You have to knock them about a bit for them to enjoy it.' She described the following conversation with a 15-year-old boy:

If she didn't want (rape) she shouldn't have asked for it.

Q   Why do you think she's asking for it?

Well look at the way she's dressed, showing tits and things.

[They are looking at a picture of what would be called a liberated woman in a well known magazine. The woman is dressed respectably in a shirt (though without a bra) and baggy trousers.]

Q   You show your tits wherever you like – no one attacks you for it. Why should a woman be forced to wear a bra?

She's doing it to get men.

Q   But even if she were doing it to attract herself a boyfriend – and what's wrong with that – does she deserve to be raped for it?

If she's asking for it – Yes.

(Lee 1983)

A girl cannot win – if she does not bother about the way she dresses she will be cast off as unattractive and unfeminine, but when she does look attractive she is in danger of being raped. This quote shows how rape, far from being the act of a psychopathic sex maniac, is the extension of the normal oppressive structure of sexual relations.

Embodied in this idea of male sexuality as natural and therefore uncontrollable is the idea that women are responsible for tempting men and by the way they dress or behave, leading them on into uncontrollable rape and violence. This concept of victim precipitation is discussed by Amir in relation to rape. He shows that quite reasonable behaviour on the part of the woman may still be interpreted as provocative by the rapist, and clothing which women may wear for the most mundane of reasons may 'invite' the man to aggressive sexual assault. Amir suggests that victim precipitation does not merely refer to a situation in which the rapist misinterprets social cues and the victim is the unwitt-ing cause of precipitating the rape. He states

If the victim is not solely responsible for what becomes the unfortunate event at least she is often a complementary partner. In other words the victim must bear the responsibility of the rapist's misinterpretation of her actions because any behaviour which is contrary to social expectations about appropriate female behaviour is open to misinterpretation. Thus if a woman doesn't reject a man's advances strongly enough, if she rejects after he believes he is likely to succeed or if she uses indecent language she is actively responsible for the impending rape.

Similarly, in another study Donna Schram (in *The Victimization of Women*) quotes men convicted of rape as saying:

I believe that women who want to be fashionable in some of the styles that are sexually stimulating to men should try and realize some of the consequences of wearing these styles before they wear them.

This tendency to blame the victim – by suggesting the woman's behaviour or dress arouses an overwhelming sexual desire which men are unable to overcome – is common in rape. It rests on two false assumptions – first, that male sexuality is uncontrol-lable and, second, that rape is about sexuality and eroticism rather than about violence towards women. Donna Schram sug-gests that the purely sexual aspects of rape are more congenial to the perpetrator's inner feelings than his basic desire to demean women. The underlying element of violence and the offender's intent to humiliate and degrade the victim is usually overlooked. Instead it is the woman's behaviour that is judged to determine the extent of contributory negligence.

Sex does not therefore take place in a social vacuum. On the contrary it is one of the most regulated forms of behaviour, circumscribed not merely by the structures and practices of the law, government and religion, but also by the ideological under-pinnings of sex–gender relations. It is only by examining the whole ideology of sex–gender relations and the place of marriage in girls' lives that an adequate understanding of adolescent sexuality and social identity can be reached.

Though feminists have produced strong critiques of marriage and the existing state of gender relations, this work has hardly infiltrated the popular marriage literature or sex education in schools. Carol Lee outlines the difficulties of even bringing up the topic of sex in many schools and the taboo on naming parts of the male and female anatomy. As I mentioned earlier, there have been very few studies of girls in education and scarcely any that focus on social relations in secondary schools. Even these throw little light on the sexual content of much social interaction. Although discussing sexuality is generally frowned upon in school, as one girl commented in a group discussion, 'You think about it all the time' (not sex in isolation but whether your boyfriend is two-timing you, whether someone is spreading tales about you or whatever). If a teacher finds 'Sandra's a slag' on the blackboard she is more likely to order it to be rubbed off than to use this as an opportunity to challenge the abuse. Female teachers need to learn to handle such comments as 'Who did you _____ last night, Miss?' but sexism is rarely taken up among the staff, where it is probably as prevalent as elsewhere. One reason for this neglect is that sexuality tends to be identified with the heterosexual act of penetration (even the clitoris may not be mentioned) rather than with all sorts of social behaviour involving erotic feelings and sometimes involving sexual harrassment. The structure of sex–gender relations and the way men and women treat each other is rarely taken up for discussion.

The narrow definition of sexuality

Even research into sexuality has usually focused on the sexual act rather than on the nature of sexual relations. It is about how people perform the sexual act, with emphasis on achieving orgasm (which many women fail to do) rather than the quality of relationships, the norms and constraints on sexual relations, the roots of eroticism. Kinsey, and Masters and Johnson revolutionized the way people thought about sexuality by focusing on what people do rather than on what they should do. They discovered that, contrary to common-sense opinion, the physiological experience of sexual arousal and orgasm for men and women was very similar. However, finding that intercourse, both marital and premarital, is far less frequently a source of orgastic release for women than for men, Kinsey assumed this was because women were less capable of sexual autonomy and had less developed sexual interests than men. Instead of considering whether women reached orgasm more effectively in other ways he concluded that:

> Whether or not she herself reaches orgasm, many a female friend finds satisfaction in knowing that her husband or other partner has enjoyed the contact and in realizing that she has contributed to the male's pleasure.

Here women's 'natural' desire to please is used as a reason for women failing to reach orgasm. The possibility that coitus may not be the most stimulating way for women to reach orgasm does not appear to have crossed Kinsey's mind. Nor does he consider the importance of sex–gender relations in determining how men and women experience sexuality (Kinsey 1953).

The main failing of Kinsey's and Masters and Johnson's research is that it does not take into account that the individuals who create social relationships and bonds are themselves social creations. As Rosaldo has suggested,

> What traditional social scientists have failed to grasp is not that sexual asymmetries exist but that they are as fully social as the hunter's or the capitalist's role, and that they figure in the very facts, like racism and social class, that sociology claims to understand (Rosaldo 1980).

Research into adolescent sexuality reflects the same reduction of sex to the physical act of penetration. Christine Farrell, in her otherwise excellent study of how adolescents come to learn about sex, regards as entirely unproblematic what the experience of sex actually is for these young people. The whole question of how sexual relations control and constrain social life is missed. The emphasis is placed on the increase of premarital sex rather than on the finding that teenagers are no more likely to have a casual sexual relationship than they were twenty or thirty years ago. As Judith Bury comments:

> Young people may become sexually active at a younger age but their sexual behaviour is still regulated by such traditional values as love, fidelity, partnership, marriage and the family (Bury 1984).

This research also indicates that far from being sexually active, girls are still expected to behave in a very circumscribed way and sex is confined to exclusive relationships. But where it seeks to go further than previous accounts is to question the subordinate position of women within and outside marriage and examine the relevance of sexuality within the social context of girls' lives. Sociologists as well as sex researchers have taken as unproblematic women's subordination. As Mary Evans comments:

It was feminism that pointed out exactly how essential women are to the family, that the whole institution rests on the unpaid labour of women and sexual division of domestic labour is closely if not intricately, related to the social division of labour (Evans 1982).

Sexuality is therefore a term that is used in many different ways and a distinction is rarely made between sex, sexuality, sexual relations and sexual division. In this study the term sexuality will be used to focus on the way that sex–gender relations are structured and how these relations permeate a girl's experience. It soon became clear that the terms on which girls participated in any kind of social life were quite different from the terms on which boys did so. Sexual reputation constantly emerges both as a cause of concern for girls and a target of potential abuse from boys and other girls. The emphasis on the importance of a girl's reputation is shown up in a whole battery of insults which are in use by both girls and boys in their day-to-day life. The vocabulary of abuse raises many questions about the construction of sexuality, the place of marriage in the girls' lives and the social organization of gender relations.

Chapter 1 focuses on the way boys and girls talk about sexuality and what this indicates about the way sexual relations are structured. The importance of a girl's reputation and the double standard of sexual morality is illustrated, drawing on material from the interviews and group discussions. The most common form of sexual abuse, 'slag', which is commonly understood to mean a girl who sleeps around promiscuously, is examined to try and throw light on exactly how the term is used. Contrary to popular belief, 'slag' often bears no relation to a girl's actual sexual behaviour. It can just as easily by applied to a girl who dresses, talks or behaves in a certain way. The only constraint on the use of 'slag' is its application to a girl who has no steady boyfriend. The chapter will explore the ways in which this leads to and reproduces a girl's subordination.

Perhaps the most significant, but not the most surprising,

finding is the absence of any form of expression of sexual desire
except in terms of an exclusive 'love' relationship. Yet there is
talk about who did what, with whom and how far they went. But
all of this talk is circumscribed and checked by the invocation of
the category 'slag'.

Far from being private and personal, sexuality reflects very
unfair power relations between the sexes. Girls are categorized
as passive objects, who can only wait and hope to be chatted up,
to be loved and not to be talked about afterwards. The terms on
which their dilemmas are handled are always socially organized
and largely socially determined.

The second chapter will focus on female friendship. Girls'
friendship groups, if portrayed at all, are seen as more intense
and exclusive than boys' groups and often polarized competi-
tively against other girls' groups. It has been argued that girls do
not go out much, do not hang around the street or participate in
the public sphere and that competitiveness of girls for boys
interferes with friendship networks.

This study shows that some of these assumptions are over-
simplifications: for example, many girls did have wide friendship networks. What is crucial, however, is that girls are not so
much excluded from the public sphere but enter it on different
terms to boys. Girls are not on an equal footing and boys obstruct
girls' attempts to take part – attempts that often end up in
girls blaming themselves for showing off or being pushy, behaviour which is related in some girls' eyes to acting like a
slag.

Finally, I shall show how conflict among girls and bitching are
often less a matter of direct competition for the attention of boys
than a defence of reputation, but at the same time reputation is
defined in terms of behaviour conforming to the 'slag' label, a
label that goes largely unquestioned but perpetuates the control
of female behaviour by males. A small group of close friends
becomes essential in a world where both other girls and boys will
openly criticize you, talk behind your back, gossip about your
every move and spread rumours. The primary demand in such
a close group is trust and loyalty. The gravest crime is to betray a
confidence. Yet the support of such a group is limited when the
iniquity of the double standard – even when related to violence
against girls from their boyfriends – goes largely unquestioned
and uncontested, and girls still blame themselves for laying

themselves open to violence or desperately produce evidence to refute assaults on their reputation.

Chapter 3 focuses on school. Education for girls is still different from education for boys. It has predominantly been directed towards preparation for domesticity (both within and outside the home) and marriage. Only in recent years has an emphasis on career been applied to working-class rather than middle-class girls. Yet even now there is a gap between girls' aspirations and achievement. Academically girls do better than boys up to the age of 16 when they take 'O' levels, but then fall behind. This chapter will show how the lowering of aspirations is a reconciliation to a life centred on love and marriage, subordination to men and restricted job opportunities. Even women who work (including professionals) see their identity as defined in terms of their relation to men rather than to work (see Gilligan 1982).

Paul Willis in explaining why working-class lads take on lower working-class jobs argues that the rejection of the school and the development of a counter school culture is a rehearsal for the realities of a lower working-class life. One way of applying this type of analysis to girls would be to argue that for girls there are a number of strategies, analogous to but significantly different from that identified by Willis, whereby girls insulate themselves from the career orienting aspects of education for lives of subordination. A second contrast with Willis is the manner in which those girls who adopt career orientations of the education system have nevertheless to reconcile these with relationships to boys and the associated pressures towards domesticity and marriage. The extent to which the experience of racism affects these pressures will also be discussed.

Chapter 4 will focus on the contradiction between the unromantic and stark picture of marriage that emerged from the girls' descriptions and their commitment – if somewhat resigned – to the idea of marriage. Most girls saw marriage as inevitable even if it involved financial dependency, domestic drudgery, isolation at home with young children and, at the extreme, even cruelty. This is less surprising when looked at in the context of the way female sexuality is socially constructed round the difference between slags and drags (one-man, marriageable 'nice girls'). The adolescent girl may sleep with her boyfriend but this does not mean that she is sexually free. A woman's femininity and active sexuality is rendered safe only when confined to the bonds of marriage and wrapped in the aura of 'love'. The very unfair way that sexual relations are structured and taken for granted throws some light on why male–female relations have changed so little.

The strategy that most girls adopt is to postpone this predicament for as long as possible or for at least ten years. As one girl said, 'marriage is something you end up with after you have lived'. In contrast to the grim picture of marriage, the years before are envisaged as providing an opportunity to have fun, to travel and to have a career rather than merely a job. The apparent contradictions between wanting to get married and postponing it, wanting a career yet failing to pursue the appropriate qualification route, and wanting to have children but seeing the isolation of mothers with children around them will be explored with reference to the constraints of their sexual subordination. Finally, the impact of unemployment on girls will be discussed.

The final chapter will attempt to draw out some of the methodological assumptions of the way in which the language of sexuality has been explored. In particular the importance of the hidden or taken for granted assumptions of the language will be shown rather than what girls may think they mean by the terms they use. The key to an understanding of the power exercised over the girls by the language of sexuality lies in the hidden or unstated assumptions of the discourses in which they participate. It is the way terms like 'slag' are actively used rather than the girls' often contradictory attempts to define them that is the object of study. It will be suggested that the effectiveness of 'slag' as a term of moral censure rests on its uncontested nature as a category and on its elusiveness and its denigrative force.

Language has to be seen as itself a material practice with its own determinate effects, rather than as an ideological reflection of other social practices. One of the most important effects is the lack of a language in terms of which girls can talk about their own sexuality and experience in a way which does not already define them as the objects of male gaze. It will be argued that it is the structure of language or discourse that contains the key to women's oppression rather than, for example, their relative exclusion from the public sphere. The chapter ends with a proposal for how language – particularly the language of sexual abuse of women – can be challenged and changed.

Notes

1 The research and early work was carried out with Celia Cowie.

References

Acker, Sandra, 'No-woman's-land. British sociology of education 1960–79', *Sociological Review*, **29** no. 1, 1981, pp. 77–104.

Amir, M., *Patterns in Forcible Rape*, University of Chicago Press, 1971.

Bury, Judith, *Teenage Pregnancy in Britain*, Birth Central Trust, 1984.

Evans, Mary, 'In Praise of Theory: The Case for Women's Studies', *Feminist Review*, no. 10, spring 1982.

Farrell, C., *The Way Young People Learned About Sex*, Routledge and Kegan Paul, 1978.

Fyvel, T., *The Insecure Offenders*, Penguin, 1963.

Gilligan, C., *In a Different Voice*, Harvard University Press, 1982.

Kinsey, A., *et al.*, *Sexual Behaviour in the Human Female*, Saunders, 1953.

Lee, Carol, *The Ostrich Position*, Writers and Readers, 1983.

Marshall, S. and Berrill, C., 'Understanding the Invisibility of Young Women', *Youth and Policy*, summer 1984.

Masters, W. and Johnson, V., *Human Sexual Inadequacy*, Little Brown & Co., 1970.

McRobbie, A. and Garber, J., 'Girls and Subcultures' in Hall, S. and Jefferson, T. (eds), *Resistance Through Ritual*, Hutchinson, 1975.

O'Reilly, Henry, 'Crisis Intervention with Victims of Forcible Rape: A Police Perspective' in June Hopkins (ed.), *Perspectives on Rape and Sexual Assault*, Harper and Row, 1984.

Platt, J., *The Realities of Social Research*, Chatto and Windus, 1976.

Rosaldo, M., 'The Use and Abuse of Anthropology: Reflections on Feminism and Cross Cultural Understanding', *Signs*, vol. 5, pt 3, 1980.

Schram, D., 'Rape' in Roberts, Jane (ed.), *The Victimization of Women*, Sage, 1978.

Scott, Marion, 'Teach Her a Lesson: Sexist Curriculum in Patriarchal Education' in Spender, Dale and Sarah, Elizabeth (eds.), *Learning to Lose*, Women's Press, 1980.

Selltiz, C., Jahoda, M., and Cook, S. W., *Research Methods in Social Relations*, Methuen, 1965.

Whyte, W. F., *Street Corner Society*, University of Chicago Press, 1943.

1 The structure of sexual relations

It's a vicious circle. If you don't like them, then they'll call you a tight bitch. If you go with them they'll call you a slag afterwards.

The concept of reputation

Boys and girls talk about sexuality in quite different ways. Though both are concerned with reputation, the basis on which it rests is very distinct. For boys, sexual reputation is enhanced by varied experience: bragging to other boys about how many girls they have 'made'. As one girl said:

A boy can be called a stud and people like and respect him – they have no responsibilities, they can just be doing what they want and if they are called a stud then they think it's good, they think it's a compliment. ... It's a sort of status symbol.

For a girl, on the other hand, reputation is something to be guarded. It is under threat not merely if she is known to have sex with anyone other than her steady boyfriend, but for a whole range of behaviour that has little to do with actual sexual behaviour.

For a boy, reputation does not appear to be predominantly determined by his sexual status or conquests. More important is his status among his mates where sporting prowess may count most or ability 'to take the micky' or make people laugh be just as vital. As Willis comments in *Learning to Labour*,

It is the capacity to fight which settles the final pecking order. It is not often tested ability to fight which valorises status based usually and interestingly on other grounds: masculine presence, being from a famous family, being funny, being good at 'blagging', extensiveness of informal contacts (Willis 1977).

Sexism appears to be one feature of male bonding, where denigrating girls and women builds up a kind of camaraderie among them. The masculine tradition that involves drinking and coarse jokes usually focuses on the 'dumb sex object', 'the nagging wife' or 'the filthy whore'. Julian Wood (Wood 1984) in his study of working-class adolescents suggested that learning to be masculine invariably entailed learning to be sexist: being a bit of a lad and being contemptuous of women just went 'naturally' together. To consider each and every woman only from the point of view of conquest, to describe women via parts of their bodies – face, tits, ginger minge (pubic hair) – is of course a reflection of the sexist ways women are depicted in advertisements and popular culture. Yet a boy knows that his reputation does not primarily rest on his sexual prowess. As Byron wrote: 'Man's love is of man's life a thing apart / 'Tis woman's whole existence.'

For a girl, the situation is quite different. The defence of her sexual reputation is crucial to her standing both with boys and girls – certainly around the age of 15 or so. The emphasis on the importance of a girl's reputation is shown up by a whole battery of insults which are in everyday use among young people. The vocabulary of abuse raises many questions about the construction of sexuality, the place of love and marriage in the girls' lives and the social organization of gender relations.

The vocabulary of abuse

The commonest insult, used by both sexes, is 'slag'. But all the insults in frequent use seem to relate to a girl's sexual reputation. It is crucial to note that the insults might bear no relation at all to a girl's actual sexual behaviour. But this does not make things any easier for the girls. An unjustified tag can stick as easily as a justified one.

Different words, of course, carry varying degrees of opprobrium. They could be used in a light-hearted way or more aggressively. Some girls laugh the insults off, others feel threatened, afraid or upset. But even if the accusations are unjustified, few girls feel able simply to ignore them or to give as good as they get. One problem for girls – if the abuse comes from boys – is that there aren't equivalent terms that they can use against boys. There are no words that amount to an attack on their whole personality or social identity. Derogatory words for boys such as 'prick', 'wanker' or 'wally' are much milder than 'slag' in that they do not refer to the boy's social identity. To call a boy a 'poof' is derogatory, but this term is not often used as a term of abuse by girls of boys. When used between boys it implies a lack of guts, or femininity: which itself connotes, in our culture, weakness, softness and inferiority. There is no derogatory word for active male sexuality. The promiscuous Don Juan or the rake may be rebuffed, as in Mozart's opera *Don Giovanni*, but his reputation is enhanced.

A girl has no vocabulary to abuse a boy with, as Jane describes when asked how a girl could offend a boy:

Dunno. You can't really say anything . . . perhaps if they go round with the girls all the time, they get called queers cos they're always with the girls. . . . You get some boys who like being in girls' company in a class, sitting with girls on the table.

It is the boys who are seen as 'feminine' and who are friendly with girls that are the only ones that are open to abuse. One teacher described how in a single sex boys' school a group of 'not real boys' or 'pseudo girls' was constructed to delineate the borders between what was male and what was female:

They are called the poofters and the cissies and are constantly likened to girls. The sexual hierarchy gets set up but some boys have to play the part that the girls would take in a mixed school. But of course they are still all boys and so the results of the pseudo girls still stand as the result of boys (Spender 1982).

It is difficult for a girl to humiliate a boy or to retaliate if she is abused. Debbie comments:

One thing I noticed is that there are not many names you can call a boy. But if you call a girl a name, there's a load of them. You might make a dictionary of names you can call a girl.

Some of these words are animalistic: dog, bitch, cow. These seem less threatening than 'slag' (or its somewhat worse equivalent, slut). She goes on to make a distinction between the animalistic names and the more abusive:

You can be called bitch, slag, slut. . . . I wouldn't like to be called some of them, but I don't mind being called a cow.

When I asked her the difference she replied:

Well it's probably that they all mean the same thing, but you can say it in a nice way or you can say it in a horrible way. Like of all of them I wouldn't want to be called a slut. If you're called a cow or a blind dog or something like that – a cow or a dog – you know you're not really that – a cow or a dog – and other people know it as well, 'cos they can see it. But when someone calls you a slut or a slag they could be one, 'cos why has the other person called her a slag or a slut? It's probably because they are one isn't it?

This distinction pinpoints what is really biting about being called a slag: that any girl is open to being categorized as a slag – any girl could be one – and if she is being called a slag might she not be one?

What is a slag?

The term 'slag' or its equivalents – 'slut', 'scrubber', 'old dog', 'easy lay' – is frequently mentioned in the various books written about boys but it has received little attention. It has been taken for granted that everyone knows what the term refers to. According to Paul Willis, 'certain reputations for "easiness" – deserved or not – spread very quickly'. The 'lads' are after the 'easy lay' girls at dances, though they think twice about being seen to 'go out' with them (Willis 1977). Here it seems that the term 'slag' or 'easy lay' simply applies to certain identifiable girls. But as soon as you ask girls to whom, and how, it is applied, it becomes clear that it is difficult to get a clear definition of what it implies from those who use it. Take Sasha's description of what she calls a 'proper slag':

I do know one or two slags. I must admit they're not proper slags.

Q   Can you describe what a proper slag is?

Available aren't they? Just like Jenny, always on the look-out for boys, non-stop. You may not know her but you always see her and every time you see her she's got a different fella with her, you get to think she's a slag, don't you. She's got a different fella every minute of the day.

Q   So is it just talking to different boys?

You see them, some of them, they look as innocent as anything, but I
know what they're like.

The implication here is that the girl who is called a 'slag' sleeps
around, but this is by no means clear, and the insult often bears
no relation at all to a girl's sexual behaviour. Whether or not it explicitly applies to sexual behaviour, the implication is that all kinds
of social behaviour have a potential sexual significance if the girl
is available – and even the term 'available' is two-edged as any girl
who is not bound up in a relationship with one man is potentially
available, for men's desires rather than their own fulfilment.
  The most pernicious ploy in the girl's eyes is when boys *make up*
that they have slept with a girl and then spread around that she
is a 'slag'. This is what Lesley referred to as a 'boy's mouthing':

It's I've slept with someone, I done this, I done that and *it's not true*.
When something's not true, that's the worst, because if it's true fair
enough – though he shouldn't say nothing – if he's so immature he has
to go boasting about it. But to lie about it, that's the worst. If they don't
get what they want they lie about it anyway, that to me, *that's stupid*.

Or Jacky adds:

Boys are boys and if they ain't got what they want, they're going to lie
about it anyway, 'cos they're show offs.

The consequences for the girl if this happens to her can be dire,
as Lesley explains:

Everyone thinks lower of them than what they did before.

The girl can of course deny the accusation and whether or not
she is believed will depend on how strong her relationships are
with other girls. But even her friends would want to find out
whether *it was true or not*. The real difficulty is proving to other
girls and boys that the accusation is false. Michelle explains what
she can do:

she could have a go at him, show him up when he's with everyone,
confront him with it when he's with all his mates, and make him feel little.

She then goes on to discuss what happened when this occurred:

Danny – this boy went out with one girl and then met another girl straight afterwards and he was meant to have said he had had both of them, and they both went at him together and really had a go at him. She told us she was shouting at him saying 'Oh you've had me then have you, funny, I never knew about it' and saying things like that. But even then it could have been true and they could have been lying. They could show him up. But he could say 'Well I did, I did' y'know, he can't prove it and he can't disprove it can he? But say she had slept with him, right, to get herself out of it she could just go up to him and say 'Oh so you've been spreading it around that you've slept with me' in front of his mates, 'but you haven't'. He can stand there saying 'But I have, I have', and they'd never know who to believe, would they?

It seems that the boy is more likely to be believed. What seems important is producing the evidence. As Sharon points out, usually the term 'slag' is used about girls you know:

... a slag is usually someone you know and you just have evidence of what they've done.

Lying can also be a problem after a break-up as Tania explains;

Like this girl that I know, this boy that she used to go out with right, he started calling her names and so all his friends started called her names.

Q   What sort of names?

Like slag, prostitute, whore, all those things.

Q   While she was going out with him?

No after she had finished with him. He went round saying that she couldn't kiss, see, 'cos she sort of gets embarrassed, she's like that over the slightest thing. He stayed with her for four months and then he goes round saying she couldn't kiss. I admit she only kissed him once but he knows that is why she wouldn't because she was embarrassed and that and he went round saying that she couldn't kiss and yet he's saying she's a slag and all. So I thought to myself how could he stay with her for four months and go round saying that. He really liked her, he would have bought her anything. It's too bad.

Here a girl who is too shy and embarrassed even to kiss her boyfriend is nevertheless called a 'slag'. The lack of connection between sexual promiscuity and sexual abuse could hardly be greater.

Any girl can be called a slag: The boys are no better at agreeing who is or is not a slag than the girls. In their book about boys, *Knuckle Sandwich*, the authors write:

The boys classified all the girls into two categories: the slags who'd go with anyone and everyone (they were all right for a quick screw, but you'd never get serious about it) and the drags who didn't but whom you might one day think about going steady with. Different cliques of boys put different girls in each of the two categories (Robbins and Cohen 1978).

So that while everyone apparently knows a slag and stereo-typically depict her as someone who sleeps around, this stereotype bears no relation to the girls to whom the term is applied. An alternative to asking those who use a term to define it is to carefully observe the rules whereby the term is used. What is important is the existence of the category rather than the identification of certain girls. All unattached girls have to be constantly aware that the category 'slag' may be applied to them. There is no hard and fast distinction between the categories, since the status is always disputable, the gossip often unreliable, the criteria obscure. If a girl does get the reputation of being a slag, all the girls interviewed agreed that the one thing she could do about it to redeem herself would be to get a steady boyfriend.

Delinquent girls, who are the ones typically ostracized as slags, sluttish or common, also reject the labels and condemn the idea of sexual easiness contained in them. Campbell, analysing the cause of fights between delinquent girls, found that it invariably came down to slurs on each other's reputation, such as 'slag', 'tart' and 'scrubber' (Campbell 1981).

What becomes important then is not the identification of certain girls but how the term is used. A look at the actual usage of 'slag' reveals a wide variety of situations or aspects of behaviour to which the term can be applied, many of which are not related to a girl's actual sexual behaviour or to any clearly defined notion of 'sleeping around'. A constant sliding occurs between 'slag' as a term of joking, of bitchy abuse, as a threat or as a label. At one moment a girl can be fanciable and the next 'a bit of a slag' or even – the other side of the coin – written off as 'too tight'. This is how a group of girls described the process:

Jenny   What I hate is when a boy tries, you go somewhere and a boy
tries to sort of get in with you and if you dislike him as a person, then
'Slag'. That's what really annoys me.

Q   They'll say 'slag' if you don't want to go . . .

Interrupted by a chorus of 'Yeah, Yeah'.

Pat   'Tight bitch', 'You tight bitch'. That sort of word.

Linda   That's a terrible thing to say to someone – 'You're too tight'.

Pat   It's a vicious circle. If you don't like them, then they'll call you a
tight bitch. If you go with them they'll call you a slag afterwards.

The girls tread a very narrow line. They mustn't end up being
called a slag. But equally, they don't want to be thought un-
approachable, sexually cold – a tight bitch.

The ways in which slag can be used

This constant sliding means that any girl is always available to
the designation 'slag' in any number of ways. Appearance is
crucial: by wearing too much make-up, by having your slit skirt
too slit; by not combing your hair; wearing jeans to dances or
high heels to school; having your trousers too tight or your tops
too low – as one girl said, 'sexual clothes'. Is it any wonder that
girls have to learn to make fine discriminations about appear-
ances and spend so much time deciding what to wear? As Tania
describes how boys look at girls

They look at people, like the trendy lot, and they think that one's been
fucked and that one's been fucked, and all that but they don't know
do they? They just say it 'cause they wanna. She doesn't necessarily have
to be does she?

Some clothes, however, indicate a lack of sexiness that can lead
to a girl being classed as unattractive:

The girl with the bell-bottoms and the beatle crushers, she doesn't get
called a slag. She doesn't get called nothing 'cause no-one thinks 'cos of
her clothes, no-one thinks that someone's had her.

Whom you mix with also counts:

I prefer to hang around with someone who's a bit decent. 'Cos I mean if you walk down the street with someone who dresses weird you get a bad reputation yourself. Also if you looked a right state, you'd get a bad reputation. Look at her y'know.

Looking weird often means dressing differently from your own group.

Behaviour towards boys is, of course, the riskiest terrain. You musn't hang around too much waiting for boys to come out (but all girls must hang around sufficiently); talk or be friendly with too many boys; or too many boys too quickly; or even more than one boy in a group; or just find yourself ditched.

Almost everything plays a part in the constant assessment of reputation – including the way you speak:

If we got a loud mouth, when we do the same they (the boys) do, they call us a slag, or 'got a mouth like the Blackwall tunnel'. But the boys don't get called that, when they go and talk. They think they're cool and hard and all the rest of it 'cos they can slag a teacher off.

Q   Who would be calling you a slag then?

The boys. They think, oh you got a mouth like an oar, you're all right down the fish market. ... They think you've come from a slum sort of area.

Or as Sophie says:

Q   What would an old dog look like?

I gotta think about that. She'll always wear tight trousers – a flirt – she'll have tight things on or short things – sexual clothes. She'll have a lot of make-up as well.

Low intelligence was sometimes mentioned:

This girl we know – she couldn't even pass her entrance into Woolworths, and usually they come from very poor families. We never ask them to go out with us.

Peter Willmott, in his study of boys, found a connection between swearing and assumed looseness. He quotes one of the boys he interviewed as saying:

You can always get a bit with the girls with big mouths, but that kind of thing turns you off after a while – you realize that if you can get it so can anyone else (Willmott 1969).

Thus 'slag' can just as easily be applied to a girl who dresses or talks in a certain way or is seen talking to two boys or with someone else's boyfriend. The point is that irrespective of whether, in a particular case, the use of the term 'slag' is applied explicitly to sexual behaviour, since a girl's reputation is defined in terms of her sexuality, all kinds of social behaviour by girls have a potential sexual significance.

There is nothing romantic in the girls' stark, indeed grim appreciation of the state of gender relations and it is here that the term 'slag' is always pivoted. A girl who is dropped is particularly vulnerable.

As soon as he's got it he'll drop you and if you take too long to give it then he drops you anyway.

Q What do you think about sex?

Oh I agree with it if you want it, I dunno, I'd hate to be pestered into it.

Q How do you think boys are about it?

I dunno the girl's always got fears about the boy going behind their backs and saying 'Oh you know, had it with her' – they've always got that sort of thing.

Q What's the fear about?

I dunno, being called an old dog or something I suppose.

Q By other girls or everybody?

Everyone, but the girls are just as bad. You say to someone 'how far did you get?' and she'd tell you and then you can always go to someone else and say 'Oh she did you know'.

What might happen after a boy drops a girl seems to be a constant preoccupation and was mentioned over and over again in the interviews. Girls describe how a boy could drop you after you've slept with him.

Then the next thing he'll be going round saying 'I've had her you want to try her, go and ask her out, she's bound to say Yeah'.

Or Alice says:

Some boys are like that they go round saying 'I've had her'. And then they pack you in and their mate will go out with you. And you're thinking that they're going out with you 'cos they like you. But they're not. They're going out to use you. The next thing you know you're being called names – like writing on the wall 'I've had it with so and so. I did her in 3 days. And I've done her 12 times in a week.'

It may not be a question of the girl actually having slept with a boy; she may land herself with a reputation as a result of going out with one boy, then being dropped and going out with one of his friends. The consequences for a girl are quite different from those for a boy:

When there're boys talking and you've been out with more than two you're known as the crisp that they're passing around. . . . The boy's alright but the girl's a bit of scum.

If a boy takes you out or boasts that he has slept with more than one girl he is more than all right; his reputation is enhanced:

If a boy tells his mates that he's been with three different girls, his mates would all say 'Oh lucky you' or 'Well done my son, you're a man'.

The pressure is on boys to boast about their sexual conquests. They have to act big in front of their friends: As one girl explains:

They might say 'Oh I've had her.' Then it starts spreading round. She might be really quiet or something and they'll say 'Oh she's not quiet when you get outside the school.' Someone else will take it in the wrong way and it'll carry on from there.

No wonder that girls have always got fears about boys going behind their backs and saying 'Oh you know, had it with her.' It is the girl's morality that is always under the microscope whereas anything the boy does is all right. A number of girls describe girls who had not slept around but had been out with a number of different boys in a short period of time 'because they were unlucky enough to be dropped by a number of boys'. This led people to start saying 'Oh God who is she with tonight?'

Sadie describes how being pretty can make a girl vulnerable:

Like Emma this girl I know – that girl's been beat up so many times over things she's never done, y'know, like she's been accused by some girls of going with one of their boys they fancy, when he's nothing to do with them. It's up to her isn't it and it's up to him, it's his preferment. And they'll all jump on her when she's been on her own, and there's about six of them. It's happened to her loads of times, it has. Maybe because she's pretty, that's why it could be, people just get jealous and that . . . accused her of being a slag when she's not.

For some girls – especially girls who lead very restricted lives and are rarely allowed to go out (from many Asian and Greek families for example) – even being known to frequent certain places was enough to risk your reputation. A Greek girl describes this process:

If at the age of 14 she starts going out, they say that no boy will want to marry her when she's older if they find out she's been going out. I know a lot of boys who would say 'I wouldn't go out with a girl that's been to so and so places.' Just because she's been to that place, it doesn't mean there's anything wrong with her. It doesn't mean she's bad. But you get a bad reputation because of the place – like some way out discos. I know a boy he goes 'If I found out that my fiancee went out to that disco, I'd leave her straightaway', he goes. Not that she did anything. It's just that y'know the place gives you a bad name even if you've only been once.

It is not only boys who call girls 'slags'. Girls are constantly accusing girls of being slags, usually when they are jealous. Jealousy can arise from the way a girl dresses or if she talks to someone else's boyfriend or if she is pretty.

Tracy's called names because they think she's too trendy. We went to this careers conference and there were loads of other schools there and we were the only sort of trendy school there. Insults were hurled at all of us, especially Tracy. It was really horrible, I thought they shouldn't be like that when they don't even know her. Just because of her clothes. ... It gets me when people say 'Oh she's a slag, she does this and she does that.' But a lot of it's jealousy 'cos they don't do it themselves. They're jealous that she's got more than them.

According to some girls teachers are also sometimes abusive:

Our teacher called this girl a stupid bitch. All she's interested in is clothes. The girl got on her high horse and walloped the teacher. She got into bad trouble. The teacher denied it.

Particular risks are run in relation to a girl's reputation if birth control and contraceptives are used. McRobbie (1978) argues that if a girl takes contraceptives on a casual date this would involve laying herself open to savage criticism because it is premeditated sex which contravenes the 'dominant code of romance', the real risk is more to a girl's reputation. On the other hand, to have sex without contraception is even more risky. As one girl explains, to become pregnant on a casual date proves to others that you must be a 'slag':

If she got pregnant then everyone thinks 'Oh my God, she really has been sleeping with him like where you can't really imagine it. If she's pregnant you know she has – you literally know it and then they say 'Oh my God, she's so cheap'. ... Then it'll just go round.

Pregnancy is the only sure test that a girl has had sex, but in any other event whether or not sex had occurred is a matter of speculation. One of the 'Sex Girls' in Anne Campbell's *Girls in the Gang* has sussed this out and uses it to her advantage:

Fuck it – I do whatever I please, you know. That's the way I am now, I do whatever I please. Even though I got to live with the people I don't care. They don't give me nothing. People say I'm a whore. They can't say 'you're a whore' just like that. They got to prove a lot of things. Even though they're talking about you, they have got to prove that. They could tell you. 'You're this, you're that.' But they got to prove it. They ain't got no proof, so what's up right. So I say, I don't live with the people no more (Campbell 1985).

How to redeem a reputation as a 'slag'

The term 'slag' seems to be accepted almost unanimously by both girls and boys to depict a girl who is promiscuous and sleeps around. However, all the girls agreed that if someone started to get a reputation, the one way they could avoid it is to 'get a steady boyfriend'. 'Then that way you seem more respectable like you're married or something.'

Sex with a steady boyfriend is not just easier to get away with, it seems to be generally acceptable.

If you had it away with your boyfriend right, and you didn't tell no-one, no-one else needs to know, do they?

The main risk then is that the boy will turn out to be a 'boaster' and will spread stories about you after he has chucked you. It is therefore unwise to sleep with a boy too quickly, in case, as a number of girls said, 'he is using you' and will be off the moment he has got what he wants. Even if you have known a boy some time it is impossible to be sure that he will not go round spreading tales about you. As Marianne comments in a group discussion:

He could have been good all the way until you went to bed with him, then as soon as he'd got that from you, he's off, just saying, had my piece from her. It's alright now and off he goes and news travels around.

Girls agreed that there were some boys who boast about it and others who don't. Debbie knows some boys are to be avoided:

One who thinks he's a Casanova – thinks he can have every bird. I know a lot of people like that. They're there rabbitting away to you about – saying I think you're beautiful all that stuff and they think you're taking it in but you're just sitting there ignoring it because they think they're Casanovas.

However they all agreed that when it came down to it you can't be sure which kind of a boy you're dealing with. Getting engaged offers some protection for the girl as a boy is considered somewhat blameworthy for having sexual relations and then ditching a girl if he is engaged to her. Becoming firmly attached to a boy is the only way to redeem your reputation.

Are class differences important in the use of sexual abuse?

As I mentioned in the introduction, after interviewing girls from two schools with a predominantly working-class intake, we repeated the study in a single sex school with a high middle-class intake. Few differences were found in the way girls describe their relations with boys and the way they categorize other girls in terms of their sexual reputation, and indeed are categorized themselves. In reviewing her study of 14-year-old girls Angela McRobbie found that there was a disparity between her 'wheeling in' of class in her report and its complete absence from the girls' talk and discourse. She concluded that being working class meant little or nothing to these girls but being a girl over-determined their every moment (McRobbie 1982). We shall see in the chapter on school that girls are aware of class differences in income, accent, access to a wider social life and better opportunities, but the power of the double standard seems as strong on all girls regardless of social class.

One distinction that did emerge in the discussions with middle-class girls is a greater awareness that the defining characteristic of 'slag' was not in fact actual promiscuity. As Silvia a middle-class girl from a single sex school explains:

There are some people I know who have slept with lots of different people but they don't conduct themselves in a way that I would call them a slag, they don't do it on purpose, they don't sort of treat boys in a completely different way – grease up to them and change their whole personality because someone they like is in the room, kind of thing, and some people who have slept with different people I wouldn't define as a slag.

Q   Why would you have defined the two girls as 'slags'?

Because they were using people and became very flirtatious. You wouldn't recognize them as the same person. You could be having a conversation with them one minute, someone they like comes into the room, suddenly they change their whole personality, they don't talk to you sincerely, it's tits out. And then all they want of the boys is to get off with them, they'd go off with two, three boys.

Q   Do you mean they'd be sleeping with three people?

Oh no I didn't mean they'd be sleeping but I mean that would be a bit hard.

The girl here is describing behaviour that would be regarded as 'natural' in a boy. It is natural for a boy to chat up girls. Here if a girl is seen to be appearing to chat up boys or perhaps to talk to three different boys in succession she is in danger of being regarded as a 'slag'.

What I am suggesting is that it is the young unattached woman who is likely to be regarded as a 'slag' rather than the sexually active girl who sleeps with her boyfriend. The term slag functions as a form of control by boys over girls, a form of control which steers girls into 'acceptable' forms of sexuality and social behaviour. It forces them into a relationship of dependence on a boy, leading as we shall see invariably to marriage. It is the unattached girl who mixes with boys but does not have a regular boyfriend who is more likely to be regarded as a 'slag'.

If you went round with someone, right, or you don't know her but you always see her and everytime you see her, she's got a different fella with her, you get to think she's a slag, don't you. She's got a different fella every minute of the day.

The following interview with Donna illustrates the way the slag categorization shifts away from girls who have settled down with a boyfriend onto the girl who is still unattached.

I don't call a slag someone who just happens to, like who desperately wants a boyfriend, so they'll get a boyfriend, then chuck her a week later, so she gets another one, so like over a period of three months, she might have been seen with six boys.

Q   So she'll get called a slag just because she's been seen with six different boys?

If you see them with a different person. This friend of ours, Brenda, like she – everyone I know, like Helen and Sally – they call her a slag. I often get so angry with them 'cos I think she's just unlucky, she just happens to go around with a group of people. She went out with one, he then chucked her, then with the other one, another boy so she went out with him and she genuinely likes him, she genuinely wants to go with him. She just happens to be unlucky enough to be dropped by them all and they're sort of saying 'Oh who is she with tonight?'

Q   Why do they call her a slag?

It's hypocritical though because I would define them as a slag at one point.

Q   Why would you define them as slags?

At one time, not at the moment, but because they've settled now with a
steady boyfriend or whatever, they think that other people are doing
what they're not doing, it's wrong. There was a time when they just
went to a party, they'd go off with some boy like and an hour later
they'd be with another, that is what I consider a slag, it's completely
debauched, sort of not really caring. . . .

As we have seen, calling a girl a slag can have nothing to do with
sex but just be directed at a girl who flirts or is seen with a
number of different boys. The reason why they are defined or
labelled as slags is as Jacky implies, that they are unattached.
Helen and Sally are no longer seen as 'slags' as they have settled
down with regular boyfriends, yet this does not stop them
branding Brenda as a slag when she is unattached. Jacky objects
to this on the grounds that it is unfair – Brenda does not fall into
her concept of what a slag is like.
  Once she is labelled a slag the language of the consumer
society emerges – it cheapens a girl if she sleeps with a boy – girls
are 'second hand' (two girls overheard a conversation between
boys baiting another boy by saying 'At least the girls we go with
ain't second hand'). Here we can see how women's bodies are not
only seen as commodities but the value of them depends not
simply on their attractiveness but also on their 'purity'. The
attractiveness of the girl is altered by having a reputation for
easiness.

If you're in a group of people, people get a reputation – she might be
quite attractive, but where a slag can be unattractive is when she gets a
reputation so if a boy wants to sleep with someone right, he'll say, 'Well
go and ask Maisie you've got a chance there'. That's where it starts
getting really awful – when you get a reputation.

Paul Willis analyses the term 'slag' as a representation: 'Woman'
who as a sexual object is a commodity that becomes worthless
with consumption and yet who as a sexual being, once sexually
experienced, becomes promiscuous. He quotes one of his lads as
saying:

After you've been with one like, after you've done it like, well they're
scrubbers afterwards, they'll go with anyone, I think it's that once they've
had it, they want it all the time no matter who it's with (Willis 1977).

What he fails to take up is the significance of the term as the location of both worthlessness and sexuality. If independent female sexuality is located in the 'slag' it is always deemed bad, since the term represents 'a dirty person', unclean both literally and sexually, and is akin to the term 'whore', thereby carrying all the connotations that surround it. The more derogatory terms such as 'slut' or 'scrubber' carry the added implication of lack of femininity. Willis, while recognizing the suppression of explicit sexuality in women, does not take up the question of why the lads fear that the opening of the floodgates of female desire will lead to promiscuity.

This idea of the danger of the unsubdued woman who will sleep with anyone no matter who it is – perhaps connects with the Latin American view of woman discussed by Octavio Paz: 'Woman is a domesticated wild animal lecherous and sinful from birth, who must be subdued with the stick and guided by the "reins" of religion' (Paz 1961). The myth that women's sexuality can be avoided by all concerned, and some sort of sexless conception – like indeed the Madonna's – will create children receives ardent support, while the assumed dangerous sexual powers of the unsubdued woman are located in the prostitute.

Such contradictory myths about the nature of female sexuality are not confined to Latin America. On the one hand women are viewed as essentially passive (as William Acton put it 'not much troubled by sexual feeling of any kind') and on the other hand their sexual desires are seen as insatiable. This dichotomy is mirrored in the slag/drag distinction. Anne Dickson suggests that these contradictory ideas – between Woman as Evil and as Chaste – are rooted in our Christian tradition. Woman as Evil is derived from the story of Eve's seduction of an innocent man in the Garden of Eden by consorting with the devil and thereby bringing eternal damnation to all humanity:

On the one hand, sex was envisaged as the devil's dynamite, a constant power in man's genitals, ready to be kindled in an instant by the tempting wiles of a woman. Or, on the other hand, the devil (and sexuality) was believed to reside in a woman's flesh; women's bodies were vehicles of evil, carriers of an evil force. Either way, women had to be avoided at all costs. The burning of a million women as witches in Europe throughout the fifteenth, sixteenth and seventeenth centuries bears grim testimony to the fear and hatred of women and their attributed powers (Dickson 1985).

However since women are also the bearers of children, the idea of Woman as Chaste embodied by the Virgin Mother emerges – the opposite of evil – and necessary in a society in which an individual's future was based on family expansion and inherited wealth. This made it crucial that fathers should be quite sure that their sons were their own. The control of female sexuality is essential. The independent sexually active woman is seen as dangerous whether a lesbian or a heterosexual. Such women are labelled as voracious, nymphomaniacs or sexless old maids.

In similar vein Stanley Brandes, in a study of sexual relations in an Andalusian town, argues that women are portrayed as dangerous and potent while men are seen as suffering the consequences of female whims and passions. All women, he writes, are viewed as seductresses and whores (*putas*) possessed of insatiable lustful appetites. When women wield their power men cannot resist temptation and are forced to relinquish control over their passions.

The teenage girl is subject to the same myths today. Concern about teenage morality is a frequent theme, shown in the controversy around the Gillick judgement. At the same time teenage girls are seen as 'easy to get' and are prey to sexual harassment, as Sharon describes:

Marion: Cos I think many girls once you're 16, 18 they think you're easy to get.

Sharon: Yes the girls put on a lot of make up and they go into the pub or something y'know nudge, nudge. She's all right. Force her to have sex and afterwards when she's pregnant abandon her and leave her alone. It's just like that.

Marion: Yeh a toy.

Sharon: Play with it and then chuck it away like it's broken.

This reputation for easiness can lead to a girl being beaten up by girls. It is often the girls who mete out retribution upon a girl who is known to contravene the dominant code of sexual conduct. Laura describes the kind of episode that can occur:

My friend knows this girl and she's a bit of a tart and she invites boys to her house and once these skinheads came along and she started taking

her clothes off and everything and these boys said they didn't
have any girlfriends but the girls were waiting outside and they brought
their girlfriends in and beat her up and everything and she was in
hospital, so now no one takes any notice of her or anything, they just
leave her to herself.

Q   The girls beat her up?

Yes, the boys as well, kicked her about and everything.

Q   What do you think about that?

It was her own fault, she shouldn't do it – it's horrible. Mind you two
wrongs don't make a right.

What is of particular interest here is the operation of an ideology
that transforms the experience of very unfair relations between
the sexes into an acceptance of those relations as *natural*. It is
somehow wrong and horrible for a girl to invite sexual activity but
somehow natural for the boy to be after it, to attempt to pester you
into it, to tell if you do and to fabricate its occurrence if you don't.
If a girl contravenes this code, she deserves to be beaten up. Fear
of getting a bad reputation stopped some girls from going out.

It makes you feel terrible, makes you feel as if you don't wanna go
out say soon as you go outside the door you get someone calling you a
slag. It's not worth it.

Contamination can also be a problem:

If someone for whatever reason has got a bad name, either your dad
doesn't approve or she's got a bad name or whatever you can't go with
that girl.
  Because you get called the same name and if you're hanging around
with a slag you must be one.

Angela McRobbie describes a teenage girl Tina in her study
avoiding a girl with a reputation:

It's always like that you know – it's not fair – but you have to watch who
you're going around with – Yet there's one up the club I'm not saying
her name but she's a proper one; she walks past and says Alright Tina.
But she's one person I wouldn't go around with cause you'd get a name
for yourself (McRobbie 1976).

The place of love

The construction of female sexuality seems to involve the construction of a difference between slags and drags: a certain kind of sexuality – essentially promiscuous/dirty in nature – is not 'natural' for all girls/women but only resides in the slag. Yet non-slags are always seen as possibly available, potential slags, until tried and found to be drags or possible wives. In other words there is always a blurring of the two categories. So what marks the difference? What functions as the location of a sexuality appropriate for nice girls? It is here that *love*, according to Deirdre Wilson, enters the picture:

The fundamental rule governing sexual behaviour was the existence of affection in the form of romantic love before any sexual commitment. For most of the girls, love existed before sex and it was never a consequence of sexual involvement.

She goes on to note, however, that:

given this threat of rejection (for sex without love) it was difficult to discover just how many girls *actually* believed in the primacy of love, and how many simply paid lip service to the ideal. Nevertheless the fact that the girls found it necessary to support this convention, whether they believed in it or not, was an important fact in itself (Wilson 1978).[1]

Nice girls cannot have sexual desire outside of love; for them sexuality is something that just happens if you are in love, or if you are unlucky, when you are drunk:

You might be at a party and someone just dragged you upstairs or something and then the next thing you know you don't know what's happening to you.

If this happens the general consensus of opinion is that it is the girl's fault:

It happens a lot. But then it's the girl's fault for getting silly drunk in the first place that she can't she doesn't know what's going on or anything.

One girl thought the only safe way was to:

watch yourself for things like that and you don't go to parties ... like you know when you've had enough to drink, you know not to drink any more. I don't even hardly drink ... I drink a few martinis and other than that I don't drink anything.

When girls talked about being in love it was often impossible to differentiate what appeared to be sexual desire from what was described as love.

It's sort of love when you want to do something when you feel something. It's sort of out there. You can't reach it. Then you often misjudge him and I suppose that's why people make mistakes. It's just a feeling you get inside you when you like being together. It's a feeling you get when you've kissed, you just get a funny feeling.

Love or 'falling in love' can be seen as both a denial and an expression of sexuality. It can also be exciting and an escape:

When you're in love you ain't got no problems.

Few girls were clear about what being in love means though invariably love is given as the only legitimate reason for sleeping with a boy. The importance of love seems to be therefore in its permitting feelings of sexual excitement while offering some protection from a reputation of sluttishness. This failure to recognize sexual desire means that girls often change their minds about whom they love:

You think you're in love and then when it finishes you find someone else who you like more and then you think the last time it couldn't have been love so it must be love this time. But you're never sure, are you, 'cos each time it either gets better or it gets worse so you never know.

You think you're in love loads of times and you go through life thinking 'God I'm in love' and you don't do anything. You want to be with this person all the time. Then you realize you weren't in love, you just thought you were. ... I thought I was in love and then I went away and when I came back I realized I wasn't. It wasn't love at all. So I finished it and I was much happier.

The girls here could just as easily be describing the way they feel attracted to a boy and then lose interest. Some girls said they had 'been in love loads of times' whereas others said they 'had never really experienced it':

It takes a while to happen. I mean it sort of dawns on you that you finally love this person. Don't think it happens straightaway. I mean you might say 'Oh look at him I love him', 'I think he's really nice' but you can't really say until you know him really well.

Given the ambiguity about what love involves it could well be that love is used as a rationalization for sleeping with someone after the event rather than, as Deirdre Wilson suggests, as always existing before 'love' could occur, which corresponds with the desirability of knowing a boy some time before you go to bed with him. The confusion that girls experience over whether or not they are in love arises from the confusion of using the word love to express what may really be sexual desire. Love is supposed to last for ever or at least for a long time, and is the main reason that girls give for getting married. The failure to distinguish between sexual desire and 'love' means that girls find it difficult to separate their sexual feelings from decisions about marriage and long-term commitment. As Fiona said:

Girls have got to keep quiet about sex and think it's something to be ashamed of.

However it is quite legitimate to talk of love. This goes some way to explain girls' obsession with pop stars. One girl mentioned that 'she used to fall in love with pop stars but now she falls in love with people'. Infatuation with a pop star was another way of directing sexual feelings into a channel that was legitimate:

There're always sort of film stars or people on TV or pop singers that girls get infatuated with. You can accept more that it's never going to happen, that it's just nice. Nice to be able to look at somebody and think how wonderful they are. Otherwise it's not a very cheering world. It makes my world go round.

The similarity between this feeling and sexuality emerges in a description another girl used to illustrate how a sexual relationship changes the way you think about a boy:

I mean one minute you think he's nice and then the next minute you'll think he's really wonderful and want to be with him all the time – you begin to see him in a different light.

Some of the more insightful girls realize the consequences of 'falling in love' and are more sceptical:

> I've got a couple of friends who are 15 and they say they're in love but I don't know if I'll ever be in love. I've had boyfriends but I don't think I've actually ... I mean the whole sort of having to live with him every day of my life would drive me mad. I think love's like a bit of a complicated thing. I think there's lots of kinds. There is love that is more infatuation where it's completely give everything. Just sort of wide eyed. Then there is love when you are able to trust someone. You'll both be on equal terms ... but to live with some ... I mean if I go and stay with friends for say three days. By the end I've had enough.

Love or falling in love is therefore both a denial and an expression of sexuality. But the only really safe place for the expression of female sexuality, as we shall see, is within marriage.

How girls are seen

We have seen that the vocabulary used to describe girls divides them into good and bad, the promiscuous and the pure, the tasty and the 'dogs'. This means that it is not only the boys that categorize girls in this way but girls too use the same categories to describe each other. Girls are seen primarily in terms of their sexual reputation rather than in terms of their human qualities, personality or attributes. Embodied in this vocabulary is a contempt for women which emerges if they are seen to be actively sexual and unattached. What is particularly pernicious about this form of categorization is that it rests on male opinion and is accepted as part of nature or of common sense by the girls themselves. When boys discuss girls this contempt not only emerges in the sexual abuse relating to a girl's reputation but also in the practice of describing girls in terms of their body parts. A dissecting approach is often taken to women's objectified bodies. As Julian Wood points out, in many of the discussions that men hold on the subject of women the assumption is that a woman can be assessed solely in terms of male opinion of parts of the female body – 'arse', 'boat', 'legs', and so on. He gives an example of a boy indulging in this favourite pastime of cataloguing the qualities of a friend's sister, who tries to persuade his friend that the girl is attractive by saying:

She's lovely, ginger minge. Oh my good God! You don't fuck the face and she's got a nice body, so what are you worried about?

The assumption is that a 'nice body' can be traded off against a presumably 'bad face'. Willis (1977) in *Learning to Labour* also describes how women as a whole are sometimes regarded by men as dirty and even evil, shown in the boys' fascination with 'jam rags' (sanitary towels). Wood describes how the reproductive and excremental aspects of the female body were constantly referred to by the boys in that fixated, disgusted tone, edged with nervousness and surrounded by giggling (Wood 1984).

In this chapter I have tried to show the way in which girls' experience of social life is constricted by the way they are defined in terms of their sexual status as female and as potential wives and mothers. Girls are described and collude in defining each other in terms of their sexual reputation. Female sexual experience is constructed in terms of male action and girls have no vocabulary or language in which to formulate their sexual experience, the very expression of which threatens their social standing. All this adds up to the need for the suppression of sexual desire if a girl is to remain respectable – unless she has a steady boyfriend.

The idea of sexual behaviour being biological rather than subject to these powerful social norms and social constraints transforms the experience of very unfair relations between the sexes into an acceptance of those relations as natural. A girl must continuously be on her guard not only of her reputation but also of sexual harassment and the unprovoked attentions of or even rape by men should she place herself in a vulnerable position by drinking at a party, or walking home late at night.

Notes

1   See Deidre Wilson's study of 13- to 15-year-old girls involved in delinquent subcultures. They saw themselves as one man girls and avoided contact with 'easy boys' who might contaminate their reputations.

References

Brandes, Stanley, 'Male Sexual Ideology in an Andalusian Town', in Ortner, S. and Whitehead, H. (eds.), *Sexual Meanings*, Cambridge University Press, 1981.

Campbell, Anne, *Girl Delinquents*, Blackwell, 1981.

Campbell, Anne, *Girls in the Gang*, Blackwell, 1984.

Dickson, Anne, *The Mirror Within. A New Look at Sexuality*, Quartet Books, 1985.

McRobbie, Angela and Garber, J., 'Girls and Subcultures', in Hall and Jefferson, *Resistance through Ritual*, Hutchinson, 1976.

McRobbie, A., 'Working class girls and the culture of femininity', in Womens Study Group, Centre for Contemporary Cultural Studies, *Women Take Issue*, Hutchinson, 1978.

McRobbie, A., 'The politics of feminist research: between talk, text and action', *Feminist Review*, **12**, 1982.

Mahony, P., *Schools for the Boys?*, Hutchinson, 1985.

Paz, Octavio, *The Labyrinth of Solitude*, New York: Grove Press, 1961, quoted in Lipshitz, S. (ed.), *Tearing the Veil*, Routledge and Kegan Paul, 1978.

Robbins, D. and Cohen, P., *Knuckle Sandwich*, Penguin, 1978.

Spender, D., *Invisible Women*, Writers & Readers, 1982.

Spender, D. and Sarah, E. (eds.), *Learning to Lose*, Womens Press, 1980.

Willis, P., *Learning to Labour*, Saxon House, 1977.

Willmott, Peter, *Adolescent Boys in East London*, Penguin, 1969.

Wilson, Deirdre, 'Sexual Codes and Conduct' in Smart, C. and Smart, B. (eds.), *Women Sexuality and Social Control*, Routledge and Kegan Paul, 1978.

Wood, Julian, 'Groping towards Sexism: boys' sex talk', in *Gender and Generation*, Macmillan, 1984.

2 Friendships

In the vast literature on the family, marriage and mother-hood friendship scarcely gets a mention. Female friendship has received so little attention that some have even questioned whether it exists or whether women are capable of friendship. Lionel Tiger, for example, considered women to lack the 'bonding' instinct that binds men together in groups (Tiger 1969). I remember arguing with my father-in-law, a bus driver for forty years, about whether women had friends – in spite of the fact that his wife spent many hours on the telephone to her friends. To acknowledge friendship among women is perhaps to give them an autonomy which many men are unwilling to allow. Friendship does however depend on a degree of autonomy and personal freedom which is constrained for most women by their family responsibilities and their exclusion from the sphere of public life.

Virginia Woolf describes her surprise when she first read a novel written by a woman portraying female friendship. 'Chloe liked Olivia. Olivia liked Chloe for perhaps the first time in literature.' She goes on to speculate on what our past might have been like if relationships between women had ever been the focus:

So often women are not seen by the other sex, but only in relation to the other sex. So common sense even dictates that women are not really capable of friendship – or at least real friendship (Woolf 1938).

The few studies of girls tend to reinforce this view – or of Simone de Beauvoir's depiction of female friendship as

rarely rising to genuine friendship ... as they all face together the masculine world, whose values they wish to monopolize each for herself ... and so in the sphere of coquetry and love each woman sees in every other an enemy (de Beauvoir 1969, p. 558).

So that McRobbie, for example, in her study based on girls attending a youth club argues that the most important aspects of their lives were both their best friend relationship and their ability to attract and compete for boys. She argues that the nature of friendship among girls was very exclusive and intense and girls did not have a wide network of friends in the way boys do. Instead of meeting in large friendship groups and participating in a wide range of activities, McRobbie and Garber (1976) suggest that girls are more home based and can be seen to form a 'bedroom culture' based on listening to records at home and talking about boys and pop-stars. This bedroom culture they describe as very exclusive of other girls and essentially 'so well insulated as to exclude not only other undesirable girls – but also boys, adults, teachers and researchers'. They quote Jules Henry who, describing American teenage experience, wrote:

As they grow towards adolescence, girls do not need groups, as a matter of fact for many of the things they do more than two would be an obstacle. Boys flock, girls seldom get together in groups of four whereas for boys a group of four is almost useless. Boys are dependent on masculine solidarity within a relatively large group. In boys' groups the emphasis is on masculine unity; in girls' cliques the purpose is shut out other girls. (Henry 1963).

It is usually assumed that these friendships will not last but will be dropped when the girl starts courting, whereas boys of course have friendships that last for life. Several questions spring to mind from this picture of female friendship: is it true that girls' friendships are invariably exclusive or do girls have a broad range of friends as boys do? What are the similarities between girls' and boys' friendships – indeed do girls make friends with boys as well as girls? In what way does the structure of sexual relations affect relationships between girls and to what extent is competition for boys a crucial aspect of group life? The first difference that struck me in comparing the descriptions these girls gave of their friendships with McRobbie's and Henry's is that although many of the girls had very intense friendships, they also participated in larger groups and knew a wide range of teenagers. As Lynn explains:

We know a lot of people who've got the same music tastes, so if we go to a gig we meet who we know have gone but not arranged to go with us. Sort of spend the evening with them;

and Sasha:

You end up knowing a lot of people. Say you're in a pub. Say you go round with a group and there's one of the group that knows a lot of people and you get to know them too. Then when you go out again you'll know them too;

or Alice comments:

Like I've got friends at school but I've still got a lot outside so it really depends if I'm out with them or my school friends. I'm glad I've got friends outside school 'cos like spending 5 days a week with the same people gets really boring.

Rather than seeking to have very intense relationships, the problem of becoming monopolized by an exclusive friendship was often mentioned as a problem to avoid. As Cheryl explains:

I'm close to a lot of people now, not just with one person in particular. I tried that out. I've had friends who you like, see them every week or more often . . . But like in the end you just . . . you just have to start lying and pretend you're going to your dad's just to go and see someone else, just so as you can see your other friends.

It is the less intense and exclusive friendships that are most appreciated, as Hannah confirms:

I can do what I like and she can do what she likes, and we've got separate friends outside school and we've got friends that mix with each other. So it's got big scope. But also, she can ring me up and I can say 'Oh I'm going out with so and so' and she'll say 'Oh see you tomorrow then'. And there'll be no resentment, she won't feel resentful or anything like that. That's what I call a close friend. I can ring her up and talk when I'm upset and she'll understand.

Claire mentions that one facet of closeness is being able to explain that you are doing something else or spend time with other friends and for this to be accepted. The analysis of questionnaires gives support to the existence of networks of girls' friendships rather than to the exclusivity of their friendships. Where we asked girls to describe how many groups of friends they had, 67 per cent said they had two or more groups and 39 per cent more than three. Most of these networks were quite large and most comprised three or more girls who all knew each other and met regularly. Other studies lend support to the important part that peer groups play in girls' lives[1] and even by the age of 12 or 13 girls have groups of friends rather than one best friend. Other studies indicate that girls also participate in groups with boys and are an integral part of adolescent gangs, not just peripheral hangers on (see Wilson 1978, Smith 1978).

To suggest that girls are always in competition for boys and that this is a main focus of their lives is exaggerated. Some girls even place friendship with other girls as more important than having a boyfriend. As Deirdre says:

I think it's more important to have friends than like a boyfriend. I'd much prefer to have my friends 'cos I mean I get on ever so well with them and we do a lot together, go and hear music, play music together and do all sorts of things.

Anne Campbell (Campbell 1984), in describing girls' gangs in New York, argues that by the 1970s the pattern of girls depending on male approval had changed and that girls in her and other research carried out in the United States indicated that girls cared more about the opinions of their own sex. She suggests that this shift may be a result of new interest in girls' behaviour in its own right or it may represent a real role change. Some girls, as shown in the analysis of questionnaires, did not have boyfriends at all and many had little contact with boys. The point I wish to make is that though some girls certainly did compete for boys this was by no means the main feature of their relationships.

One reason why girls have been regarded as secretive and locked in exclusive groups is that researchers have encountered difficulties in interviewing girls. McRobbie and Garber mention the hostility that they felt when interviewing girls in a youth club and describe how the girls constantly made jokes among themselves 'for the sole purpose of confusing or misleading the researcher who may well be infringing on their territory by asking personal questions or whose presence at the weekly disco they resent'. They none the less put this down to the exclusivity of girl culture, whereas it seems much more likely to be a result of resentment towards the researchers impinging on their leisure time, perhaps without convincing them of the value

of the research. In this project girls were interviewed and group
discussion took place during school time and provided a welcome
diversion from classes. Under these conditions girls spoke freely
and spontaneously about their lives. Girls' groups may be
smaller and less fluid than boys' groups but it is important
to bear in mind that there is considerable variation and flux
between and within girls' groups too.

They do, however, usefully ask whether the invisibility of girls
is due to the dominance of male sociologists (many of whom
have manifested a particular fascination with the 'macho' image
of male groups) or to the specifically masculine nature of most
subcultures. Others have argued that youth culture is pre-
occupied with the problems of masculinity to the neglect of
femininity. If girls are absent or only peripheral to what is
essentially a male phenomenon dominated by masculine con-
cerns, they ask whether there is an equivalent female
youth collective experience producing its own strategies;
whether there are complementary ways in which girls interact
among themselves and with each other to form a distinctive
culture of their own:

When the dimension of sexuality is included in the study of youth
subcultures, girls can be seen to be negotiating a different space
offering a different type of resistance to what can at least in part be
viewed as their sexual subordination (McRobbie and Garber 1976).

Yet even if girls do not participate in boys' groups and their
public activities and stay listening to records with a close group
of friends, this is not a form of resistance but is, if anything, an
adjustment to their expected feminine role which, by and large,
is anticipated to centre on the home. Girls do of course go out
and enter into social activities but, as we have seen, they do so on
different terms from boys. For example, McRobbie argues that
one reason the street remains taboo to women is made clear by
the disparaging term 'street walker'. However, the term 'street
walker' does not necessarily ban them from the street but pro-
nounces the terms on which they can be seen on the street, i.e. as
girlfriend or slag. In other words, the girls' appearance on the
street is always constrained by their subordination. The term
slag is one of the ways through which their subordination is
effected. This is why, rather than regarding girls' activities as

a resistance, their participation in social life should be seen primarily as a product of gender subordination. There is evidence that some girls do go out a great deal more than McRobbie's research suggests and are involved in leisure activities. One study of delinquent 14–18-year-old girls found that sixty-one out of the sample of 131 went out five or more nights a week (Smith 1978). Similarly, the Scottish Council for Research in Education found that from a sample of 15-year-olds in ninety-seven Scottish schools, in general it was girls that took more part in leisure activities than boys. The exception was games, where 74 per cent of boys were involved, compared with 57 per cent of girls (SCRE 1970).

If many girls do have a wide of range of friendships is it true to say that their friendships are different in quality to boys', and is their participation in outside activities significantly curtailed? I shall first consider in what ways girls conceptualize their friendships and relationships with boys. Debbie depicts the difference between girls' and boys' friendships in this way:

The boys always try to act up to each other. They always seem to act tough. 'I'm more manly than you' they say. Girls are much more sort of matey with their friends ...

and the similarity: 'They both want to get their laughs and their kicks.'

Having fun together was important, as Christine describes:

I think we found it giggly to go up to an old lady and say something to her and then run away. We went through a stage of knocking on people's doors and running away, that sort of silly game. I think it was 'cos we were bored. And all of us were making out we were getting on the bus or something and then make the bus wait for us and then nobody got on. .... You do it all the time and you all know what is going to happen.

And Sandra describes fun in this way:

When you're having a joke, that is fun. Me and my friends go out at the weekend we just feel so sort of free and without any compulsion to do anything, that you could just be happy and be mad, just walk along the street, happy and giggling and saying stupid jokes and just laughing 'cos you're happy and it's just nice to be free.

Apart from having fun, almost all the girls described their close friendships as very intimate, where their innermost thoughts could be aired:

I mean you can talk to each other really well and when you're upset they really are helpful. You come in in the morning and burst into tears and they just make you laugh or they chat to you.

We never have real arguments. You sort of ring them up and they're there and you can talk to them.

Your friends help you along. Like I had trouble with this boy see and you know something happened and we started arguing and my friends helped me along in proving him wrong, they always seem to give me the right advice. I always take it and it always turns out right.

These quotes illustrate the centrality of *talk* in girls' friendships. To speak about their experiences seems to be girls' main means by which they handle the world. This is not to say that girls just talk while boys act. But the overriding activity is talking: what happened, who said what, who wore what, what is going to happen.

Talk about boys [laughter] you do though, clothes, records, where you're going – boys – what else do we talk about? Girls we don't like – tarts.

Johnson and Aries make this point about the importance of talk in adult female friendship:

The substance of women's friendships ... close female friends converse more frequently than close male friends about personal and family problems, intimate relationships, doubts and fears, daily activities. Male friends, on the other hand, discuss sports more frequently than female friends. Adult women also report greater depth of discussion with their female friends about personal problems, family activities, and reminiscences about the past; men report greater depth in conversations with same-sex close friends about the topics of work and sports (Johnson and Aries 1983).

Girls describe talking as helping them 'sort out your mind', whereas when you are alone you get to feel 'desperate', 'depressed' and 'confused'. Talking to friends seems to be the main way that girls cope with the gossip and innuendo about their 'reputation' and a way of defending themselves against unjustified insinuations. Seen in this context, no wonder the quality that is universally considered to be most important in friendship is trust and loyalty. Elizabeth describes a true friend as someone who will not spread round what is told in confidence:

I probably trust her the most of anybody and she trusts me. I mean of course people have told me things that they don't really want anyone else to know and I've told someone else and everybody does that. But something that Jane tells me I couldn't tell anyone else. Something that I told her, I hope she couldn't tell anyone else.

She goes on to distinguish this from being close to someone, which does not necessarily involve trusting them:

Like Nicky and me are very close but I couldn't trust her at all. I don't think she could trust me either. We're basically not very alike. She doesn't really know how much something means to me when I tell her something and I mean she's very bitchy behind my back.

Zoe has a similar concept of friendship:

I think I just trust them in everything, the deepest secrets, every experience you've been through and it's just understanding both ways.

If ya tell on someone you'd probably be called a snide, you wouldn't have no friends left and they'll go round telling things about you that ain't true.

Q Called a what?

A snide. It means you tell someone something you're not supposed to tell, you promised not to.

Listening uncritically to your friend is a crucial aspect of the rapport. Many of the friendships the girls described had lasted almost all their lives – since they were two or three or at least from primary school:

I've known her since I was four. I can do what I like and she can do what she likes, but we've both got each other.

Janey did not think, however, that everything could be shared:

There're always a few things which people keep completely to themselves. But not much 'cos I don't really have any problems which I can't tell anybody.

Other girls expected more than loyalty – sticking up for you was also important:

To be on your side rather than someone else's – even if they don't agree. If you have an argument, your friends stick up for you even if she doesn't agree with your point because she's your friend.

Maisie considered this extension of loyalty going too far:

I think your mate should keep out of it if she disagrees. But if I really don't agree with some of what my friends say, if I don't agree, I don't stick up for them.

Where to draw the line and risk a severe disagreement with a friend was a problem which fortunately did not arise very frequently as friendship usually rested on a high level of consensus:

Quite often if you're such good friends there's a lot of things you agree on so it doesn't usually arise – a situation when you totally disagree with your friend.

You can't argue with a friend.

I mean if you argue and they go off and they never speak to you again, they're not really a very good friend.

Being able to withstand a disagreement could be regarded as a facet of strong friendship.

Boys do of course talk as well, though sociologists tend to denote them as 'hanging around' rather than investigating what they discuss. As Kay describes it, talk is not an activity that is considered manly:

I think most boys do talk as well. But they won't admit to talking the same as girls. I think boys aren't supposed to talk to each other but they do. I mean Kev has his mates round and may first talk and gossip the same as what girls do.

Boys' talk is ignored and girls' talk has been trivialized as gossip and chit chat. Its importance in developing intimacy and cohesion between individuals and groups remains uninvestigated. As for men to express feelings about relationships or emotions generally is considered unmanly – bravado and denial of vulnerability and sensitivity lead to the derogation of women and at the extreme to violence and sadism.

Bitching

Friendship is therefore characterized by loyalty and sticking up for your friend. The other side of the coin is bitching and spreading gossip and rumours. Bitching is constantly referred to as something that girls are particularly adept at and as the source of aggravation and even fights among girls. Sandra explains why she can talk to Emma but not to Sue:

I think I can trust Emma more. Sue, one moment she can be really nice but the next moment she can be really bitchy. Sue will use what you say against you. But I wouldn't tell either of them anything really secret.

Reading these accounts it becomes clear that girls fear that their so-called friends can rarely be completely relied on not to gossip. Girls are regarded as far more bitchy than boys and many girls see bitchiness as an inborn characteristic of girls – as part of their 'general character'. Boys on the other hand are described as more straightforward and honest.

As Lynn said:

They're more honest, they'd sort of fight it out, whereas girls just say things behind their backs,

and Sandra:

There are boys that bitch as well – but on the whole I think girls have got more character for bitching.

Anna goes so far as to say she prefers to talk to boys:

Girls get ratty and annoyed with each other and say things about each other. Whereas boys are more outright. They don't bitch about each other behind each other's backs so much.

Bitching is not, however, only betraying confidences but typically involves calling other girls names and often casting doubt on their reputation. Sexual abuse can be used in what is described as a joking way or more viciously:

Friends are bitchy to each other in a joking way. We always keep calling each other names but we don't mean it.

When asked how you could tell whether someone was joking, Cathy replies:

You can tell by their face, you can tell by the way they say it. 'Cos when we say it we sort of say something like 'You bitch' and start laughing but then other girls just look at you or give you a dirty look, call you a name and walk off. They can't stand there and face you – they say it when they're walking past.

What is crucial for the girls is not so much what you say as the way you say it. All girls are therefore described as bitchy, but some are more nasty in the way they bitch. Bitchiness can refer to two rather different types of behaviour. On the one hand it is used to describe friends talking about you behind your back rather than to your face. As Mandy explains:

If you get annoyed like if a group of you went out and one girl was being really stupid all evening, and started getting really annoying then quite often you wouldn't go up to her and say 'Hey listen, you're being a stupid idiot'. You'd go home and you'd sit with your friend and say 'God, wasn't so and so being a real cow. God she's really getting on my nerves and I wish she'd shut up.' And it builds up from there. . . . You go on about other things she's done – finding fault.

Here bitchiness seems to be a way of devaluing aspects of other girls that you wish to signal as 'not you'. It is a way of marking differences between other girls and yourself. Sally describes this succinctly:

Like I am bitchy. I say 'oh she's so fat'. You say it in front of friends for instance to see if they say 'You can't talk, you're just as fat' or to see if they agree with you.

A more vicious type of devaluing aspects of other girls is to cast doubt on their sexual reputation, which is why much of the bitching characterized by girls involved sexual abuse. Jennie, for example, pinpoints what is meant by bitching in this way:

What people say when they bitch. They say they think some girl's a slag or something like that.

If rumours spread about you it can be unnerving, as Anna comments:

If it undermines my own confidence to such an extent that I start feeling uncomfortable then yes it bothers me. And if it isn't true, if it's false, it also annoys me if no one had a nice word to say about you, it's going to upset you. I must say I get quite paranoid.

Judy had stopped going to discos in London because all the girls were bitchy, shouted abuse at her and made her life a misery. She describes what upsets her:

The main thing that comes to mind is 'Look at that slag' or something like that ... I don't think most of them know the meaning of the word really 'cos calling someone a slag you've got to really have proof haven't you? I don't think it's very nice but it does upset you, it starts me thinking that why are they saying it to me. I don't go after boys all the time but I like to enjoy myself.

According to Denise, girls who wanted to have a boyfriend but have difficulty in attracting boys are the most bitchy:

There's a group of girls who hang around together and pretend they're not interested in boys but really are, like would really love a boyfriend but can't make the step. They get a bit bitter and say 'Look at that one, silly slag.'

Or those who want to attract attention:

They do it to attract attention, they want everyone to look at them. Lots of girls they say it to everyone to make them think they're hard. Boys are going to think they're tough.

In these examples bitching seems to be used as a way of putting other girls down and differentiating the 'slags' from oneself – it is a way of protecting your own reputation.

Other girls use the term bitching to describe a betrayal of confidence, which is what leads Betty to consider it unwise to share all one's problems with anyone:

There're always a few things which people keep completely to themselves. I wouldn't tell them family problems. That's not to do with them, it's just between family. It's best to keep that to myself. I wouldn't spread it around 'cos you can't always trust friends. Just tell them things that don't really matter but help you to relax. . . . Some of them talk behind your back. You tell them something. That's why you have to be careful who you hang around with, who you speak to, 'cos even the slightest thing you tell them, they can change what you've said and get you into a lot of trouble. You might say something to them 'Don't tell anyone what I just told you.' The next moment the whole school knows it.

If you do [tell confidences] you'd probably be called a snide and you won't have no friends left and they'll go telling things about you that aren't true.

The most risky confidences centre again around sexual behaviour and feelings. One reason why so few girls talk even to their closest friends about sexual desire or actual sexual behaviour is through fear that their friend might betray them and gossip – spread the rumour that they were a slag. There is no parallel for boys to the risk of this betrayal which can destroy a girl's whole social standing. True, a boy can be called a poof but the rumour of whether or not he has slept with a boy or not would not circulate salaciously in the way it spreads around with a girl. Girls do not discuss which boys are poofs in the way boys discuss who is a slag. Boys have less to betray in regard to other boys' confidences, as their reputations are not based solely on their sexuality. They may agonize about whether their relationships are going well, but the social impact of their sexual behaviour is quite different. The slag categorization and constraints on a girl's sexuality act as a very effective way of restricting both the expression of a girl's sexuality and her freedom of action – her independence. The term poof or queer and milder terms such as wanker are used as slang but are not censures on the expression of sexuality in the way slag is.

Friendships with boys

Some girls do not only have different networks of girlfriends but also know different sets of boyfriends. Jenny has so many friends that she finds it really hard to think of having a party as this would involve inviting so many people that it would be 'completely manic':

I go swimming and I've known them since I was a baby and I grew up with them and they're just like my brothers, there're no girls there of my age ... then there're my other friends who might clash because the lot at the swimming club, they're more pampered by their mums – like my mum calls the other lot ruffians – Oh but they're not, they've just not been so pampered like the swimming club. They go swimming while the others would be in the pubs. I've got a mixture of friends. It's really hard if you're thinking of having a party and they might not get on.

Many of the girls think that friendship between girls and boys is no different from friendship within the same sex group and that it is really important to form a friendship with a boy before embarking on a sexual relationship. As Lucy explains:

I think a boyfriend who isn't a friend isn't really worth having – it's best if you know them first 'cos if you meet someone and it's like start going out with them straight away you don't really have time to develop a friendship. Whereas if you meet someone and you're just friends with them before you start going out with them, then there are things that you can talk about to a friend and things which you talk about to a boyfriend, but when these are combined, that's really best.

Another girl, Jacky, describes her relationship with her boy-friend in these terms:

We used to talk about everything really. Just everything you talk about to a mate you talk about to him. 'Cos I know him inside out really. Every trick like.

Other girls, however, had little or no contact with boys and none mentioned a boy by name when asked who her friends were.

Fighting

To depict girls as spending most of their time at home, talking and listening to records, is incorrect. Girls do go out though parents, realistically in view of the risks of girls being molested or raped, are more concerned about how girls are to get home and who they are with. Girls frequently mention that their parents insist on their being home by a certain time, and want to know who they are with. This does not, however, mean that girls do not go out – they visit pubs, gigs, discos, clubs and the flicks and do pursue a wide range of interests. Many play musical instruments – which makes one wonder why so few women play in orchestras and bands later on – go to football matches, go swimming, ice-skating, or hang around the flats, often in mixed groups of boys and girls. The belief that girls do not participate in groups is challenged by Lesley Smith's study of a sample of delinquent girls, who were active in such groups as Skinheads, Greasers and Hell's Angels. Girls participate in drugs, drink, sex, fighting and crime (Wilson 1978, Smith 1978, Campbell 1981). Girls are on the street:

I reckon we fight as seriously as the boys. You know, if anybody comes up to us we'll smack a bottle in their faces ... any Greasers or Hairies come in (our territory) and there's trouble ... I always carry a knife or a bog chain when I go down there (Skinhead girl, quoted in Smith 1978).

There can be little doubt about the seriousness of their group involvement, not only in social activity on the streets but in fighting also, as shown in this incident which Maureen outlines:

I've got a friend who – she's walking home one day at about 5 o'clock and three girls came up to her and they were skinhead girls – and there was like park railings and they banged her head against them – she was walking down the road not doing anything.
  You get them in a group and it's a power thing, they feel safe when they're in a group, and it's like the image of skinheads. I mean I'm not saying that every single skinhead – of course not and probably most of them wouldn't demand your money or threaten you with knives – not if they were alone. But you get kind of press-ganged into doing it when they're in a group.

Here the same dynamics that have been portrayed in male youth studies are at work.
  Tracy describes how she bunked off school with a group of boys and they'd break into cars and steal speakers and car radios or anything that was left in the car. This was 'good for a laff'. (She would only discuss this when the tape recorder was turned off.)

Street fights are described by several girls. Girls are much more of a threat than boys:

I'm really scared of girls – walking down the road – girls will hit you where boys wouldn't. You know you can get away with a lot more with boys than you can with girls.

Some girls describe quite violent incidents, like Sandra:

I was walking home with Jenny, and these girls just started picking on us and everyone hit me and then they started hitting her. I went to help her and they started punching and smacking me about. It was out of order. I really hate that. They hurt me and cut me in the face. They booted me in the leg and Jenny was in tears. She had a mack on and skirt. They ripped her mack and they gave her a bruise. . . . There was no cause for it. We were only walking from school to the flats.

Q   Why did they do it?

Just jealousy. I mean she did look nice. If you had a burberry and it's expensive ain't it? She had one of them on and 'cos they said to her 'What do you think you're doing here?' She goes 'We're walking through the flats.' And she didn't mean it but it sounded cocky but she weren't. And they just went 'You're not allowed to walk through these flats, this is our territory', and things like that. They don't even live there, but I do.

Frequently, how a girl is dressed and what her appearance conveys – her sexual attractiveness – seems to be grounds for a fight. How you look someone up and down can lead to trouble:

I had a fight with a girl. The way . . . she used to look at me as if I was real dirt. So I went mad one day and hit her. It gets me when they laugh at you. I think they've got a nerve. You go out and try and pay a lot of money for nice clothes and they go and sit there and take the mickey out of you. That gets me.

Another incident at a big conference on careers was described by several girls. Jane was fuming after it:

I can remember I had burns up my legs from having cigarette butts thrown at me and I walked out. I thought if I had a bomb I would happily drop it on them. I'm not prejudiced against anybody really, but that kind of thing I just hate. 15 and 16 year old girls who just don't know you and just make presumptions.

Allegations about your sexual reputation – often involving sexual abuse – frequently lead up to a fight. Anne Campbell (1981), in her study of delinquent girls where she surveyed 251 16-year-old girls from working-class areas of London, Liverpool, Oxford and two areas of Glasgow, found that 89 per cent had participated in at least one fight. Questions about who had made the last remark before the fight revealed that the most commonly offered reason was that slurs had been put on their sexual reputation, such as slag, tart or scrubber – often false accusations against the girl and insinuations about their sexual morality. She concludes that although girls' fighting is strikingly similar to boys', girls did not fight in groups to defend either their reputation or their territory, nor did they 'seek public arenas in which to demonstrate their bravery'. What she does not appreciate is that an attack on a girl's reputation is an attack on her personal morality and integrity which only she can defend. She is isolated in her defence. She cannot demonstrate that she is 'respectable' by a display of bravery – only by convincing her attackers that she has not slept around. The trouble is that there is no way you can provide evidence, as Sally explained:

You can't tell a slag from seeing someone walk down the road. I mean you might see a girl walking down the street looking really debauched, sort of a mess, make-up's run everywhere, but you don't know the reason. You might call her a slag but I mean she could have just been beaten up by her boyfriend – you don't know the reason. You should have evidence before you call someone a slag.

Fights between girls are therefore less fights over boys or boyfriends in any direct sense, than fights over personal reputation and integrity. It is this that makes them ambiguous and difficult to resolve: 55 per cent of Anne Campbell's sample had no idea who had won in fights between girls. A reputation cannot be clearly and unambiguously redeemed even by physical victory in the same way as it can either by a boy proving his 'bravery' or, for that matter, a clear competition between girls for boyfriends. But, ultimately, the very vacuity and ambiguity of the term 'slag' is, as I have argued, a reflection of its role in the control, by males, of girls' freedom.

Sometimes, of course, competitiveness does play a part. In this incident, boys were drawn into a dispute between two girls and led to the boy being thrown out of a top window and ending up in hospital. This supports Cheryl's view that fighting often arises when a girl has a grudge against another for fancying her boy-friend or being too popular with boys:

A very good example happened two weeks ago. This girl Jane never really mixed with us fourth years, she used to mix with the fifth years. Then this new girl came to the school, Sadie, and Jane realized that all the fifth years were paying more attention to her so she just went around telling everyone 'Sadie's a slag – she comes from this other school that's really rough.' She had this grudge against Sadie 'cos the boys were giving her more attention than they were to her so Jane and Sadie had a fight, 'cos Jane was going round saying Sadie was a bitch. Jane comes up and starts fighting Sadie because she was standing next to John. Then Jane and her mate ran off and got some really big boys and next day they came to school and she accused John of hitting her and holding her down and scratching her face. So John got beaten up and he got kicked through the window, a top window, dragged out of here and kicked through the window. He got two or three bottom teeth broken in the gum, kicked in the face, he got really squashed ... a couple of stitches in his hand, a busted top and bottom lip. All for jealousy. ... The guys who kicked him through the window were taken to court.

By no means all the girls approved of fights and some regarded them as childish. Rebecca comments:

I hate to see girls fighting. It looks stupid. Girls like to scratch more and try to get each other's hair out, they don't punch.

But what is important is that girls are as involved in fighting or in inciting fights as boys. This serves to make the problem of violence in schools much greater than is commonly realized. While bullying and fighting by boys are recognized phenomena (St John Brooks 1984), investigation of the extent of girls' involvement in such activities has yet to be seriously undertaken. What is clear however is that girls' involvement in fighting is very much associated with conflicts over sexual reputation. Any attempts to deal with it therefore will not get far if they fail to tackle the root causes of violence – the domination of male conceptions of sexuality and the ways in which they lead girls into relations of competition and antagonism.

Dropping girlfriends

Few girls drop their girlfriends when they start going out with a boy, though this may happen when they leave school. Chris Griffen's research (1985) indicates that when a young woman started going out with a fairly regular boyfriend, she gradually lost touch with her girlfriends often at the young man's insistence. She concludes that this 'deffing out' process was even more prevalent after young women had left school because they did not have the daily contact with girl friends at school.

The girls in this study are younger and still at school, so their friendships do not appear to be discarded in the way Chris Griffen describes. Some girls do not think their friendships are affected by going out with boys, though this clearly is a concern. Janet, in talking about her friend Rebecca, says:

I think sometimes she feels that perhaps I'm not sharing as much with her as I do with him, but she doesn't make much of it. But I know I do. They're both on equal terms. We often go out as a foursome.

Some girls describe their feelings as changing:

Since I've been going out with Brian they don't seem to be the same. It seems to be the same thing they talk about all the time. I enjoy myself more with him.

Yet this girl's friends have not started courting, so perhaps she has less in common with them.

If girls do drop their friendships it is important to examine why and what constraints are placed on strong female friendships. It does appear that it is difficult to maintain friendships once one is tied with young children at home. Dorothy Hobson outlines how much married women with young children miss their friendships and the freedom to go out when they want and wondered whether they would make the same choices to get married and have children – if they could have those choices again (Hobson 1978). The burden of child care which falls so heavily and exclusively on the mother, often unsupported by wider kin and the wider community – leaves her little opportunity to keep up her friendships and go out with her own friends. A young woman with children is lucky if she has any free time at all. This is, however, not because women are incapable of friendship or because friendship is not important to them. It is due to realistic constraints on their freedom, where the idea of the woman having a night out with her friends is not accepted in the way a night out with the boys is regarded as natural. Hannah Gavron (1966) found that 25 per cent of working-class wives in her sample had no friends at all and many middle-class wives felt they were becoming isolated. Brown and Harris, in their study of depression, did not even consider the importance of friendship, but concentrated on women's intimate sexual relationships and participation in work. It is, however, a mistake to see women's depression as a product of poor sexual relationships although this may be one facet. The lack of contact with other people coupled with the almost non-existence of a social life or leisure activities participated in by women outside the home may be just as important (Brown and Harris 1978).

When women do get together, in factory life, for example, it is often friendship and solidarity between the women that makes the tedium of the work tolerable. Sallie Westwood illustrates how friendship is an essential part of life on the shop floor:

You get friends here who keep you going, so you say 'It's not so bad, really. ... ' The things that happened vary from scurrilous gossip to organized pranks, but they were given life through the network of friends – There were no 'laffs' to be had on your own: bunking off to the toilets, spending too much time in the coffee bar made no sense if it was an individual activity. There was no way to organize a prank without your mates or to have a laff at a pornie picture or a coarse joke. The material base for all of these was the friendship group (Westwood 1984).

She shows that friends were supportive both inside and outside the factory, but whether this applied to women after they had left to have children is doubtful.

If a friend dislikes your boy friend this can best be put as Miriam describes:

If it was a friend that I really valued it would affect me a lot, 'cos I consider that more important than a boyfriend. But if it was just a friend, not one of my really amazing good friends, I'd probably just probably tell them to shut up.

Miriam went on to say that if she refuses to go out with some boy who wants to go out with her and her friend said 'Oh he's so nice', this wouldn't make any difference:

That's happened quite a lot but I usually don't. I mean it makes me think about it but usually I say, stop trying to fix me up.

It's a man's world

Girls do not – at 16 – necessarily drop their friends when they start to go out with a boy, but on the other hand the expectation is that a girl will attach herself to his friends and his pursuits. Jeanette describes what happens:

Usually a girl will end up drinking in some pub that her bloke has always drunk in. Blokes – they'll always keep with their friends – that's one thing I've noticed. Blokes can go out and stay with friends whether they're going out with a girl or not, but if the girl's going out with a bloke, she drops her mates and then picks them back up when she stops going out with him.

Social life is now centred round boys and boys' activities – the pub is a male environment where girls may go with their boy-friends but do not often feel confident to go on their own or in a group of girls. This means that for boys their social life does not alter very much, whether they have a girlfriend or not – they are still welcome round the pub or can go on their own to a disco without the risk of being harassed or called a 'slag'. Without a boyfriend, a girl's social life is restricted. Many girls hesitate to go out on their own – even if they have parental approval – or even with a girlfriend, and their hesitation is based on real risks. The terms on which they participate in pub life are different, and to drop into a pub would be interpreted differently for a girl and for a boy. It is often the boy who decides where to go and it is he who holds the purse strings (part-time work for boys is much better paid than baby-sitting for girls) and when girls do go out they often go out with older boys:

Some boys think they're flash because they've got a bit of money and think they can buy you. I said to one boy 'Ditch your money' and he wouldn't let me so I thought 'He thinks he can just do what he wants.'

Girls are not expected – nor often allowed – to buy their round at the pub, indicating their subordinate status, and if challenged, as Martha recounts, boys 'get the hump', 'because they think it's degrading', and complain if a girl buys a round:

That annoys me. Even when you're not going out with one of them in the pub and they're just your friends, 'Wanna drink?' and they go 'No' and if you get them one they'll go 'Don't want it' and you just say 'Oh shut up. You've got it now' and you give it them and they get the hump. They go on the turn some of them. ... Because they're boys. Boys are meant to be men, manly y'know. It's just not right for a girl to buy a man a drink.

Buying a drink for a man puts a girl on an equal footing with him, which many men find hard to tolerate. Girls described how they were ignored or expected to sit quietly, while boys discussed how many girls they had made with their mates:

The boys you hang around with are mostly the same: like they'll be talking about other girls all the time, they won't talk about what you've been doing, they just talk about what girls are bad and where they've been.

Q   In front of you?

Yeah. Like if you're sitting down and there's a whole crowd of boys talking about a girl and you'll be stuck there on your own and you say 'I might as well go home'.

No wonder that many girls thought pubs were one of the most boring places.

Quite often girls described the way boys talked about their friends in quite explicit sexist terms:

They talk about some of our mates horribly, the ones they know, really good friends, they say they know for a fact that they are a slag because – say they're five of of them she's been passed around. Then they'll talk about her. They say awful things anyway, whether it's true or not. Even when you're walking down the street they'll scream things at you.

Boys treated girls quite differently when they were with their pals, according to several girls:

They don't take any notice of you when they're with their mates.

Or they take the mickey out of you.

A boy who would treat you quite reasonably or even be friendly with you when on his own, would treat you with disdain when with his friends, as Jenny describes:

We got a crowd round here near the flats. When they're with their mates, they're all hard and they call you all the names in the book. But when they're on their own they talk to you. They say 'Hello Jenny, how are you getting on at school?' or 'I like your glasses.' but then when they're with their mates, it's 'Alright goggles' and all the rest of it. That's what makes me sick. They're not like it when they're on their own. They only want to act big when they're with someone.

This behaviour, if shown by a girl, would of course be described as 'being bitchy', but since it is boys' behaviour, it does not get characterized in that way.

The girl is always blamed

Girls generally regard the girl as responsible if she allows the boy to behave in a chauvinist manner – gravely underestimating the relatively powerless position she is in.

I think like in a relationship with a man it's really up to you and if you're going to let the man you're with walk over you, do what he likes, go out with his mates and you have to sit at home, well on the whole it's your fault 'cos you're a person and you can get up and say 'No I want to go out. I want to do this. I want to do that.' When it comes to jobs, it is unfair, the pay and other things, but when it's like a man and woman relationship – it's both people who've got to try. Like I know people who'll say they've rung up Tony or whoever and he says 'Oh I'm going out with me mates' and they'll say 'Oh well' and they won't go out. I think that's wrong. Why should you sit at home waiting for someone when they've gone out having a good time? Either you should say 'Oh I think that's really very nice' – or in looking for a boyfriend you want someone who's not going to go off with his mates and expect you to sit at home.

On the one hand this girl puts the blame on a girl who stays at home while her boyfriend goes out with his mates or lets a boy 'walk over you', but on the other hand she ends up by admitting that it's a good idea to look for a boyfriend who's not going to go off the whole time and expect you to stay at home. What she fails to mention is the constraints on girls having a good social life without boys – the few places they have to go without being molested, difficulties of getting back late at night and greater control over them by concerned parents. She is already putting the blame on girls for their social oppression.

If a girl is blatantly sexually harassed and denigrated, this is often written off as unpleasant but just 'boys having a bit of fun'. The taken-for-granted insolence of boys is evident in many accounts:

Like this boy was calling me a bitch. I don't know what he was calling me a bitch for. He was picking on me. 'You bitch' he goes. He knew my name. *He just wanted to make fun* or something 'cos he had some friends round there. He comes up to me and he says 'Hello sexy'. I goes 'Who are you talking to?' He goes 'You'. ... I was scared and 'cos my friends were there we just walked off. So stupid, fancy calling someone a sexy bitch.

What is most tragic about this episode is the resigned way the girl reacts to being blatantly sexually harassed. She is scared and upset but she writes his behaviour off as merely stupid rather than insulting and threatening. The boy is not criticized for his behaviour: his chauvinism is regarded as 'natural' or something that is unalterable.

In similar vein, his infidelity is viewed differently, as Jessie recounts:

It doesn't seem so bad for a boy. It seems natural for a boy when you think about it [laughs]. You just think it's normal but for a girl it ain't.

Q You don't think it's normal for a girl?

No, I think in the end girls end up to be prostitutes and I think that's wrong.

Similarly, in looking at the reactions of girls to being hit or beaten up by their boyfriends, the most common response is for girls to blame the girl rather than condemn the boy's behaviour. Excuses are often put forward for why the boy should have behaved in such a way – many bordering on the idea that perhaps the girl provoked the attack. On no occasion does a girl decry the prevalence of violence from boys; it is taken as 'one of those things that is unchangeable.' Not that you should put up with it, though. Witness this discussion:

Sandra: If someone hit me I'd turn round and strangle them.

Jane: And me.

Sandra: I cannot understand people who stay with men who hit them.

Zoe: Some people like being slapped.

Hannah: Some people do, though. Some girls say 'Oh he hit me last night' and I say 'Did you hit him back?' And they say 'No'. Then I say 'Are you still with him?' and they say 'Oh yes'.

Sandra: I don't like that. I hate seeing boys hit girls.

Hannah: I wouldn't stick with anyone that hit me.

Even these girls, when discussing why a boy hits his girlfriend (or a husband his wife), do not condemn it outright and blame the boys – rather the blame is placed on the girls for putting up with it. Excuses are given for the boys:

Sandra: They do it without realizing it.

Jane: Sometimes someone really gets hysterical, they get annoyed and go 'Shut up, shut up' and that's it.

Sandra: I think what probably happens with like husband and wife: they'll start an argument and he doesn't *mean* to hit her really, he doesn't want to hurt her, it's just like the last resort.

When Jane objects to her boyfriend kissing another girl, and is hit by him, she still excuses his behaviour:

We just shouted at each other and he walked out after hitting me, but he had too much to drink anyway, but we got over it.

Other excuses for boys becoming violent are presented:

If a boy can't stick up for himself he comes to you, just because you're a girl. He says 'You've been telling my mates I can't stick up for myself', and he hits you just to prove it to his friends. But he can only hit a girl 'cos he knows the girl wouldn't hit him back.

Excuses for boys' violence appear without any condemnation of the boys' behaviour, and range from 'he doesn't mean it', his friends are bullying him and he needs someone to take his anger out on, he has had too much to drink, to 'being provoked beyond endurance' and even 'the girl likes being slapped'. The only recourse the girl seems to have is to break off the relationship, which opens her up to the 'slag' categorization, as we have seen in the first chapter. Violence is largely condoned by the community and rarely seen as a product of the very unfair relationships between the sexes. It is rarely condemned as unacceptable and women frequently refer to a woman as 'provoking' a man into violence. This stems from the acceptability of machismo and the general denigration of women.

Although some girls condemn violence the boy is never blamed. It is the girl rather than the boy who is criticized for putting up with the boy's behaviour.

Conclusion

So what generalizations can be made about girls' friendships? It is important to understand the mechanisms whereby relations between girls are dominated by their gender. This domination can be both direct and indirect. Writers like McRobbie have looked for direct mechanisms: girls don't spend much time in public places, but retreat to a 'bedroom culture' as a form of resistance, because boys dominate the public spaces and the streets. Another direct form of domination is argued for by McRobbie, when she says girls form only exclusive relations and do not involve themselves in broad friendship groups because they are in competition for boys. Obviously, if girls were spending most of the time seeing other girls as potential competitors for boyfriends, then large stable friendship groups would be difficult to hold together (McRobbie and Garber 1976).

The conclusion of this research is that these direct mechanisms can easily be exaggerated. Bedroom culture is probably less a 'culture of resistance' carving out an alternative space to the public spaces dominated by boys, than it is a simple rehearsal for women's role in later life. It therefore does not exclude entry into public spaces and participation in large friendship groups. Although competition for boys is an aspect of girls' relationships, it does not dominate them to the extent that large open friendship networks are precluded. Girls' relationships are dominated by their gender much more importantly through indirect mechanisms which govern *the terms* on which they enter into and participate in friendship groups. These mechanisms surround the overriding predominance of 'slag' as an ever present force, censuring and constraining behaviour irrespective of the presence or absence of boys or whether the girls are in actual competition for particular boys. 'Slag' is present as sexual censure even when boys are out of sight and out of mind. Such is the power of male dominance that its exercise is not dependent on the presence of the oppressor.

I have given three examples of the power of slag in action. First, the conflicts between girls over reputation. A girl's reputation is defined in terms of her sexuality, whether or not she is a slag. I have shown how difficult it is for such conflicts to be resolved, precisely because they are quite independent of conflicts for particular boyfriends which would, of course, provide some 'objective' (!) resolution of such conflicts. Second, for a girl to go out independently, to buy drinks for boys or drop in to a pub for a drink is to risk the label of 'slag'. For her to wander round the streets at night or enter into public life on the same footing as boys is impossible – she is constricted in her freedom of movement in a way which neither she nor boys appreciate. Third, I have shown how even when boys are present and engage in chauvinist or violent behaviour they are in fact marginalized from the discussion of such violence, a discussion which focuses overwhelmingly on the behaviour and responsibility of the girl. In understanding the role that 'slag' plays in determining the relationships between girls, I am reminded of the concept of power as 'self carried' which has been elaborated by Foucault (1979), a power of male dominance which is not 'exercised' by boys over girls, but which girls carry with them and which penetrates their lives and their recreations. But there comes a point at which the power of male dominance is felt to be directly exercised by men and begins to break a girl's autonomy and her links with her own friends. This point is reached when girls start going out regularly with boyfriends: where the long and lonely march through the institution of marriage and family life begins.

Notes

1   Delamont, Sara, *Sex Roles and the Schools*, Methuen, 1980; Lambert, R., *The Chance of a Lifetime*, Weidenfeld and Nicolson, 1977.

References

Brown, G. and Harris, T., *The Social Origins of Depression*, Tavistock, 1978.

Campbell, Anne, *Girls in the Gang*, Blackwell, 1984.

Campbell, Anne, *Girl Delinquents*, Blackwell, 1981.

de Beauvoir, Simone, *The Second Sex*, Penguin, 1949.

Delamont, Sara, *Sex Roles and the Schools*, Methuen, 1980.

Foucault, M., *The History of Sexuality*, vol. 1, Allen Lane, 1979.

Gavron, H., *The Captive Wife*, Penguin, 1966.

Griffen, Chris, *Typical Girls*, Routledge and Kegan Paul, 1985.

Henry, Jules, *Culture against Man*, Random House, 1963.

Hobson, Dorothy, 'Housewives: isolation as oppression' in Women's Studies Group, CCCS, *Women Take Issue*, Hutchinson, 1978.

Johnson, F. and Aries, E., 'The Talk of Women Friends', *Women's Studies International Forum*, vol. 6, No. 4, 1983.

Lambert, R., *The Chance of a Lifetime*, Weidenfeld and Nicolson, 1977.

McRobbie, Angela and Garber, Jenny, 'Girls and Subcultures: An Exploration' in Hall, S. and Jefferson, Tony (eds), *Resistance through Rituals*, Hutchinson, 1976.

SCRE, *A Study of 15 Year Olds*, University of London Press, 1970.

St John-Brooks, C., 'The School Bullies', *New Society*, 6 December 1984.

Smith, L, S., 'Sexist Assumptions and Female Delinquency: an Empirical Investigation' in Smart, C. and Smart, B. (eds), *Women, Sexuality and Social Control*, Routledge and Kegan Paul, 1978.

Tiger, Lionel, *Men in Groups*, Thomas Nelson & Sons, 1969.

Westwood, Sallie, *All day Every day*, Pluto, 1984.

Wilson, Deirdre, 'Sexual Codes and Conduct' in Smart, C., and Smart, B. (eds), *Women, Sexuality and Social Control*. Routledge and Kegan Paul, 1978.

Woolf, V., *Three Guineas*, Penguin, 1938.

3 Marriage

I don't want to get married until I've had my life

Marriage has never been more popular – over 90 per cent of both men and women marry at one time or another. The average age has risen slightly in recent years, standing at 22 for women and 24 for men; but cohabitation before marriage has increased: in 1979–81 over a fifth of women marrying had cohabited with their husband beforehand. There is, however, no evidence to suggest that cohabitation is replacing marriage and only 3 per cent of adult women aged 18–49 are cohabiting.

Though marriage is so popular, divorce has steadily increased. The number of divorces annually in the UK doubled between 1971 and 1982. This means that one couple in four can expect their marriages to be broken by divorce within twenty years. For those with children, if present trends continue, one child in five will see their parents divorce before the child reaches the age of 16. Changes are therefore occurring in the family, and in 1979 one child in twenty was living with a step parent and just over one in ten with a lone parent. (The proportion of families with dependent children headed by a lone parent increased from just over 8 per cent in 1971–3 to over 12 per cent in 1980–2).[1]

This study was carried out in an inner city area where the rate of family breakdown was rather higher than the national average. Fifty-two of the sample filled in questionnaires about their family circumstances. Over half of these, thirty-two, were still living with both parents. Of the remainder, fourteen were living alone with mum (one of these was a widow), three lived with dad and stepmother, three lived with mum and stepfather.

The prevalence of marriage and the tendency of divorced couples to remarry is usually interpreted as lending support to its success in providing couples with a secure and romantic future – the 'they lived happily ever after' of fairy tales. What seems to be left out of this picture is that for young people there is little alternative to marriage if they want to lead an active sex life without moral censure. In this chapter I shall argue that active sexuality is only rendered safe when confined to the bonds of marriage and wrapped in the aura of love. The idea that it is natural for a girl to marry and the emphasis on falling in love deflects attention away from the very unfair way that sexual relations are structured.

Pearl Jephcott, in a study of 17 to 21-year old girls published in 1942, found that two things dominated their lives. First, their homes and second, the extent to which future marriage appeared to occupy their thoughts throughout adolescence. Practically every girl said she wanted to give up her job when she got married, none thought her job was more important. When Diana Leonard in her research in Swansea in the early 1970s asked girls when they had decided to get married, they said they could not remember a time when it had not been a consideration. Any relationship without marriage in mind was unimaginable. Rather than choosing not to get married, girls *fail* to get married (Leonard 1980). Sue Sharpe (1976) in her study of over 200 girls from the fourth forms of four schools in Ealing in the 1970s found too that 82 per cent of them wanted to marry – a third of them hoped to get married by the time they were 20 and three-quarters by the age of 25. They accepted that a husband and family were the most satisfying things in a woman's life. According to Jessie Barnard, it is the discrepancy between this ideal and the reality that leads women to experience shock which emerges as depression and despair. She believes that marriage makes women sick:

There are 2 marriages in every marital union, his and hers. And his . . . is better than hers. While for centuries men have been told – by other men – that marriage is no bed of roses, a necessary evil, a noose, a desperate thing, a field of battle, a curse . . . it is men who thrive on marriage. Despite all the jokes about marriage in which men indulge, all the complaints they lodge against it, it is one of the greatest boons of their sex.

When one looks at the mental health of wives in Barnard's report the picture is grim. The statistics vary from country to country, but overall the people most likely to suffer from depression, who are likely to have breakdowns and be dependent on drugs – are wives. She reports that poor mental health is greater among those whose occupation is a housewife than among any other occupational group (Barnard 1973).

In a study carried out in the 1970s of the social origins of depression in Camberwell by Brown and Harris a similar picture emerges. They found that two in three married working-class women with a child at home were suffering from clinical depression or were borderline cases, compared with 17 per cent of a cross sample of all women in the study. Married working-class women were at a higher risk of depression when they had young children at home. Working-class husbands were likely to fail to recognize the difficulties of child care, which they saw as a cushy job; this trivialized the women's work and lowered their self-esteem.[2]

Others have also argued that husbands seem to benefit much more from marriages than wives do. Single males are four times as likely to be in mental hospital than are married males of the same age. Married men also are healthier than unmarried males of the same age. Married men are also healthier than married women and single men. For men, marriage offers material advantages which the boys recognize. As Spike, in Paul Willis's study, says:

I've got a right bird. I've been going with her for eighteen months now. Her's as good as gold. She's fucking done well, she's clean. She loves doing fucking housework. Trousers I brought yesterday. I took 'em up last night, and she turned them up for me. She's as good as gold and I wanna get married as soon as I can (Willis 1977).

In contrast, girls describe marriage as offering no such material advantages but rather a greater burden of domestic labour. Thus although the modern view of marriage encompasses ideals of equality and sharing, there is little evidence that these have led to a greater division of housework and child care among married couples. Even among middle-class couples, where greater equality might have been expected, evidence of domestic violence and the rise in the divorce rate suggests little in the way of change.[3]

The contradiction between marriage as an ideal and as a reality emerges in this research. Almost all the girls in this study took for granted that they would get married, yet when you look at the various kinds of comments they make, what is portrayed is not so much a romantic as a realistic view of the grimmer aspects of women's lot in marriage. As Jenny says:

I think that once you get married you lose pride in yourself really.

Q   What about boys, do they lose pride in themselves?

The ones I know, they don't really lose pride because they sort of go out, they don't have to wear a ring or anything do they? They still go around free as though they weren't married.

They saw marriage for women involving the shouldering of a domestic burden that carries little in the way of status and rewards:

My dad won't do anything, he won't make a cup of tea, he says he does the work for the money and the rest is up to my mum – she does part-time work too.

Gina puts it this way:

The wife has to stay at home and do the shopping and things, she has got more responsibility in life and they haven't got much to look forward to .... We've got to work at home and look after the children till they grow up, you've got to go out shopping, do the housework and try to have a career. Then the man comes in and says 'Where's my dinner?' when we've been to work. They say 'You don't work'. It's because boys are brought up expecting us girls to do all the work. They expect their mums to do it and when they get married they expect their wives to do it. They are just lazy.

Marriage also involves a financial dependency that is both a constriction on mum and a bone of contention between mum and dad:

My dad won't give in like. My mum she sort of goes short, now and again, and she asks him for extra money and he just won't give it to her and I think other families are like that. If you don't have to rely on a man they don't feel so tight with their money.

What is mentioned most of all is the isolation of being at home. Such comments as:

If you stay at home, you get bored and lonely;

or

My mum hates being at home you know but she has to stop working because she's going into hospital and she's going to hate that – she's going to be so bored.

Q   Is that why she works?

Yes, she just don't like being at home.

Work often envisaged as a career rather than just a job is seen as some kind of salve to these grimmer aspects:

I want to get married, I don't want to stay single but I also want a career. If you marry and it's just the man who goes out to work ... I would want to go out to work, I wouldn't want to be stuck in the house because then that's just – that's just like a woman's job, really being stuck in the house.

or as Anna says:

I'd like to work as well 'cos I'm used to being on my feet. I can't stay home in the house. I mean I could cook and that lot – I would be glad to do it, cooking and so on but not stay at home all day, like looking after kids – I couldn't do something like that.

It is the women who do not work but stay at home all day who in Brown and Harris's study are the most prone to depression. It is not simply that women suffer from isolation in the home but that they are forced to accept treatment that no employer would get away with:

My dad thinks she should be a total wife mother image, be there ready and waiting. The meal should be ready and if he clicks his fingers she should go running. And when I see him doing that it really infuriates me and I think I'd never – if I ever got married – I'd never marry anyone like that.

Or Tracy said:

I don't want to get married and have people bossing me about telling me what to do. From the experience of my mum and dad getting married I just don't think it's a very good thing.

Their comments were scarcely romantic but depicted marriage as wasting your life.

Sometimes I look at my parents and just think they're so stupid. I see them together and they never seem to want to go out. I think they have such a boring life. My mum does everything for my dad and I reckon my dad's real selfish. He's like a kid. But I just look at them and I think I never want to be like you, have a wasted life. 'Cos they married when they were – my mum was 17 and my dad was 19. So they've been tied down ever since – My mum had a kid immediately.

Boredom was however a relatively minor complaint compared with some girls' descriptions of married life. Illness was frequently mentioned:

Like my mum has back pain, she gets it all the time, and my dad says 'Oh it's nothing'. If my dad had it for a week it would kill him 'cos he – men – don't go through so much.

Beatings and cruelty were also referred to and several girls described the boy they would want to marry as one who 'did not beat them up'. Sandra thought beatings were usually associated with drinking:

I will get someone who doesn't like drinking a lot and just has a little coke or something.

Q   Is it common for men to come home drunk?

Yes, it's like this lady round our flats, she gets beaten every night because her husband goes drinking, comes home about twelve, starts beating her you know for nothing, saying she's been out with this man, she's done this and done that, he just makes it up, any lies and starts trouble.

Or Mandy says:

There's one thing I don't like about men do to their wives is beat them up. At least that's what it's like with the next door neighbour. She's married and they're her children and her husband when he comes home at night he beats her just for the fun of it and then he wants to go to bed with her afterwards . . . . I don't want that if I get married.

Some families faced severe problems – Barbara described how her father who had at one time been a psychologist had had frequent nervous breakdowns which meant her mother not only had to work full time but also had to look after him through his breakdowns:

It must be awful to think that you've wasted your life getting married to somebody like that. She's just stuck with him now and forever unless he gets better or gets a great deal worse and has to be taken into hospital.

In view of the high rate of divorce, this was often put forward as a reason for avoiding marriage, though it rarely led girls to discard the whole idea:

If you look at our homes it's not such a good idea – there're so many people's parents who are divorced. It's about 50 per cent of marriages just fall apart.

Girls whose parents had separated often expressed distress:

It happened to me not last November but the one before. I live with my dad now. They just decided to separate and we worked it out. But for about a month I walked around crying even in lessons.
  You feel really unwanted. You feel like 'Oh they don't care about you. They just care about what they feel themselves.' I felt so depressed because I dunno it's the sense of failure.

Feeling uncared for was a constant theme:

My parents got divorced when I was about 2 and I've always felt they don't care about me. They just care about themselves. I always think people are against me. It's horrible.

Other girls accepted divorce with greater equanimity: Deborah put her mother's failure at marriage down to her disinterest in housework:

My mum's been married twice, once my first dad left when I was about 3, but that wasn't – I mean none of the marriages have been bad sort of 'taking to court sort of relationships'. You have to go to court but they've always been decisions made together. It's just that my mum, my mum is so untogether about housework, she really wasn't made to be married. She's much better off by herself. I'm more sort of together about housework and money and things. She's terrible with money and it's caused problems with my second dad because he was quite the opposite and it caused a clash. I still go to my second dad every two or three weeks and we get on fine. I'm going on holiday with my first dad and his wife and my friend Jo. We get on all right too.

Overall the girls' view of marriage is not romantic but seems to be realistically based on their observations of their own parents, relatives and acquaintances. What needs to be explained is why the girls wanted to get married and how they came to terms with or rationalized the negative aspects of that predicament.

No alternative to marriage

The most important reason girls put forward for getting married is that they do not see any realistic alternative. As Tracey puts it:

This idea of love and marriage. I think you're all broken down into thinking you're eventually gonna get married and have kids, you know. If you're really ugly or in a right state or something then you're not going to – you're not going to go out and meet a bloke – it's like that.

The choice of getting married then becomes a negative one – of avoiding being left on the shelf with all the opprobrium attached to the spinster. As Lee Comer expresses it:

A whole battery of neglect, suspicion and derision is directed at the non-married and the childless and they are stereotyped as shirking their duty, selfish, immature, lonely, bitter, abnormal and unattractive or pathetic (Comer 1974).

The horrified responses of parents who are told by their sons or daughters that they are gay or lesbian are depicted in a recent survey published by the London Gay Teenage Group. One 16-year-old said:

Her [my mother's] first reaction was 'You'd better go to the doctor about it.' This was followed by 'How disgusting, keep away from me' – as if homosexuality was contagious. Now she thinks that just because I like girls, I must either hate men or want to be a man (neither of which is true). I think she's hoping that I'll grow out of it, but I can't see this happening (I don't want to either) (Trenchard and Warren 1984).

Occasionally girls do mention sharing with other girls:

I might get married about 20. I'd live with my mates first.

However this is almost always seen as a temporary transition. The only safe place for the expression of female sexuality is within marriage. Engagement offers some protection for the girl as a boy is seen as somewhat blameworthy for having sexual relations and ditching a girl if he is engaged to her. But life as an independent, unattached woman is always open to risks:

If you don't want to get married and want to live a free life and you go out with one bloke one week and another the next, everyone will call you a tart, like you've got to go out with a bloke for a really long time and then marry him.

It is not just the constraints on an independent sex life that leads girls to marriage but that the family is seen as the 'only hope we appear to have for the fulfilment of needs for warmth and intimacy and love' (Smart 1984). Lesbian relationships can of course offer these, but only if the girl manages to face the pressure towards conformity and, of course, is attracted to other girls.

However, for most girls lesbian relationships are not on the agenda. The choice is seen as one of being on your own or getting married – what Adrienne Riche has named 'compulsory heterosexuality', the 'great unacknowledged reality'. In the absence of choice, she argues, women will remain dependent on the chance or luck of a particular relationship and will have no collective power to determine the meaning and place of sexuality in their lives. The choice girls have to make is painfully expressed by Julie. When asked if she wanted to get married she replies:

Yeh I want to. I'm scared to sleep alone. I'm too scared of the dark. I shouldn't like to live all alone. I wouldn't like to live with my family all my life but I wouldn't like to live alone either.

Being on one's own holds fears for many girls – some related to the harsh reality of existing in a male dominated world where you need protection. Girls can never go out on their own – or even with girlfriends – without fear:

A boy can go out and just enjoy himself but a girl can't really, she's got to worry. Old men come along and molest you. I don't like going out. You feel safer if you go out with other girls than go out on your own. You're even safer with a boy, that's what you feel whether it's true or not.

Q   Even if there're two girls do you feel scared?

Yes. You could be walking down a dark alley and you always think someone is following you. If just one man pounces on you, you just kick them somewhere.
  My brothers sometimes go out late because they go to work and then go out in the evenings, my mum and dad go to the pub and I just sit at home and watch TV. Sometimes you wonder if life's worth living.

The fear of being sexually harassed places real constraints on a girl's freedom and is another reason why getting a boyfriend holds attractions. A boy is often seen as lending protection to a girl:

Say you have a boy protecting you. It's as if no one can hurt you or nothing. You're protected and everything. If someone does something to you, then there's him there and it just makes you feel secure.

Q   What do you need protecting from?

He doesn't like it when other people are out to get you. It doesn't mean that other people can't do nothing to you but it's kind of protective toward you.

The need for protection emerges in a number of interviews. Charlotte, in describing how her brother is treated differently from her, attributed this to his ability to protect himself because he is a boy:

Boys are a totally different physique. I could go out and I could be raped whereas he couldn't. He'd have more chance of protecting himself. I think that comes up the whole time. It's not that a boy is more trusted. It's that he's freer.

Girls are often reminded of the reality of rape by the experiences of their friends:

I wouldn't walk home after 11.30 pm on my own 'cos I've got two friends who have been raped and that really did terrify me. But then it sort of wears off. Before you know it you are walking around late at night, it's frightening. I do get worried about it all the time.

In one of the most popular novels of the 1970s, *The Women's Room*, the main character Mira realizes that the dice are loaded against a woman going out on her own. She is going out with Larry and is in love with him but is unwilling to sleep with him as she knows that would risk pregnancy and marriage. She realizes that the qualities she admires in Larry are the same qualities that would make him a disastrous partner. He abandons her in a bar because of her refusal and she dances with his friends, has too much to drink and narrowly escapes being gang banged by them all. It is then that she realizes that she can never be free.

She could not go out alone at night. She could not in a moment of loneliness go out to a local tavern to have a drink in company. .... She could not even appear to be lacking an escort, if that escort decided to abandon her she was helpless. She couldn't defend herself. She had to depend on a male for that. .... She averted her eyes from any male who passed her and never smiled at them even when they greeted her. .... Her dream of choosing and living a life of her own had vanished (French 1978).

Living alone is too difficult and frightening for a girl and except for a small number of middle-class girls the choice of sharing with other girls is financially impossible. Cohabitation or marriage becomes the only path away from living at home (except for the few who go on to higher education). The contradiction between the ideal of living with someone you love and being driven into marriage by loneliness comes out in Meg's comment:

I couldn't get married or live with someone I didn't love, and I couldn't live on my own I don't think either. I've always got to have someone there. Even if it's someone I can't stand. I'd rather have someone there than no one. I don't think I could live in a flat or a house on my own. I just need someone there.

For most girls the only way of leaving home is to get married, even if it's to someone they can't stand! While at home, it is very difficult for them to experience any kind of independent sexual life without the double standard coming into operation and aspersions being cast on their morality. The idea that when a girl gets married she is exercising 'free choice' does not take these structural constraints into consideration – she has neither the financial independence, nor the cultural support to make other choices. If she avoids boys she is either regarded as 'too tight' or as a lesbian – or both. If she seeks an independent sexuality she is labelled 'a slag'. This study illustrates the processes at work in making heterosexuality compulsory rather than a question of free choice.

Delaying marriage

In the face of these strong pressures to marry, girls inevitably subscribe to the idea that they want to get married. Nevertheless, their realism about marriage, based on the observation of their parents that we have already noted, leads them to devise ways of rationalizing or cushioning its inevitable impact. Almost all of the girls want to put marriage off for some time, usually about ten years. It is important to bear in mind that ten years when one is 15 seems a lifetime away, as one girl put it:

I don't think about the future at all until it happens. I don't think – Oh what am I going to do in ten years' time for a start. I never think that. I've never thought that in my life. I think 'What am I going to do tomorrow?'.

By delaying marriage, many girls think they will be able to have some fun, often fantasized as travel and seeing the world. Marriage is something you end up with after you have lived:

I don't really want to get married 'cos I want to go round the world first like me dad did. ... They got married when they were 30 years old, they just sort of *had their life first* and then they got married and had us, but when you're an air hostess you don't start the job until you're 20 so I want to work until I'm 35.
   I want to have a good time before I get tied down. Meet different people, travel the world.

Some girls want to delay marriage in order to have time to become qualified to avoid ending up in a dead end job. Once embarked on a career, some girls predict that children will not interfere with their work:

I'd like to get married, but not until I'm about 27, or late twenties, early thirties, you know I'd like to get really started on a career.

Q   What about when you get married?

That wouldn't mean giving up my job or anything, no.

Q   What about if you had children?

That wouldn't, I mean obviously I'd look after them for a few months, but I'd get back to work as soon as I could.

Other girls realize how constricted mothers' lives can become, but see this as a woman's fault rather than as a reflection of the lack of support for child care:

I want to get a start in a good career or whatever. I want to live, have a nice good fulfilling life, before I actually settle down and. ... It really annoys me the way people just like give up the second they have a child, give up working, just give up everything ... they become a housewife and I never want to do that.

Some girls recognize that their desire to embark on a career could be stalled by marriage – which could just 'happen' as Helen suggests:

I'd like to think that I'd get a job but you never know 'cos my mum, she could have gone to university but she got married. It just happens doesn't it? But I'm more ambitious than she was – I mean I would go mad if I didn't have a career.

Thirty years ago the idea of combining work and marriage was unusual and radical. Margaret Stacey described in a letter to Elizabeth Wilson how things were in the 1950s:

The point for me – and I can't have been the only feminist to have this view although we had no movement when I graduated – was that the women older than me chose either a career or marriage. You couldn't have both we were told ... (But) we said, I and my friends, we would be mothers and women in our own right' (Wilson 1980).

In the 1950s and 1960s working-class women began to return to work to enable their children to have the opportunities they had never had. Jephcott describes how few options young working-class women had and how jobs, rather than being chosen, just 'happened'. She quotes one woman as saying:

> They kept asking you what you'd like to do and I kept saying I'd like to work with children and they kept saying 'Wouldn't you like to work in a factory?' and I ended up in a factory (Jephcott 1945).

Few girls seem to have grasped the reality of the level of youth unemployment, though some do realize that they will have little choice, unlike smart girls:

> The smart girls – most of them want to be secretaries, go to typing school or whatever. Some want to go to university. We all want to do different things – like some might want to work in a shop or be an air hostess – I want to do tap dancing but I wouldn't mind working at Marks and Spencers. They don't give much money but it's a good job. You get a discount on everything.

Girls who do want a career often realize that relationships with boys might upset their intentions and therefore steer clear of them:

> If a boy does ask us out we say 'No' don't want to know, because we want a career and go round the world and all that lot. So we just leave them alone ... we talk to some boys and they always go around with girls, so if they (the girls) see us they start calling us names and it will aggravate us and we would not be able to get on with our work, so we just tell them (the boys) to go away.

Or as Haylee puts it:

> I don't really bother with boys now – just get on with my homework. I go out with my friend and then go back home. I was brought up not to like boys really 'cos I've heard so much about what they do – robberies, rapes and all that, so I keep away from them.

Q   What do you mean – brought up not to like them?

> Well my mum told me never to go with them because they're bad and they damage your health and things like that, don't know

what she meant, but she says they ruin your life if you get pregnant, she said it's best to keep away from them, so I do.

Some girls see an advantage in not growing up too quickly:

I think there're a lot of decisions to make which I really don't want to make at the moment so I'd rather act childish so I don't have to make the decisions.

Boyfriends and marriage easily interfere with career intentions and disrupt girls' work – they see what happened to their mums and how little autonomy they have.

Choosing the right man

Another way of attempting to avoid the predicament of marriage – apart from putting it off for as long as possible – is to attribute the unhappiness that they see in marriages around them to the wrong choice of partner. The subordinate position that many women find themselves in is often attributed to their lack of good sense in choosing the wrong husband rather than to the general structural constraints on women at home with young children. Love in terms of finding a man who will understand them, share things with them and protect them from the loneliness they see around them is seen as a solution. What they seem to be expressing is the hope that love will save them from the grim reality of most of the marriages they observe. What husband you pick is what matters. This group discussion illustrates the way one girl reconciles herself to marriage which the other two girls see as offering nothing but disadvantages:

Q   What do you think about marriage?

Mary: I think it would be a bit boring.

Alice: It will be a bit boring but no one knows, we don't know what it will be like till we get married.

Mary: Well it's just like your mum's isn't it?

Alice: But not all marriages are like that though are they? Like if your mum's goes bad, yours might go good, it's *what husband you pick.*

Hazel: My mum's life is so boring.

Mary: 'Cos all they do, is the mum cooks the dinner, mum goes
to bed with dad, the mum gets up in the morning and cooks
breakfast, cleans the house, and that's it, that's all she does all
day, every day.

Alice: My mum goes to work but some men expect women to
stay at home.

Hazel: Stay indoors crunched up on a little seat doing knitting.

Mary: You feel your mum is stuck at home having a hard time,
it's boring. They're closed in.

Alice is right in one respect. Some men allow women more
autonomy than others. She does not however criticize the unfairness of the marriage deal itself.

The contradiction between aspirations and reality often
emerged:

Jacky: Quite a few girls say 'I'm going to marry for money.' I
say if I had a man it's going to be for true love. Other people
think I'm stupid but I don't think it's stupid. If you marry for
money you like half the person.

Q What do you think true love is?

Jacky: I think when you agree on most things and you're both
the same in your ways. I don't see it very often but it's important
to know that you are going to agree 'cos if you disagree then
there'll be rows and arguments. When I think of some boys,
they're going to boss the girls around and they'll swing in circles.

Q What about working?

Jacky: Oh yes. I would hate to rely on a husband. I see how my
mum depends on my dad and it's turned her against him. I'm
not going to marry a husband like my mum did. My dad he
doesn't help at all. I don't know what they see in each other.
They must love each other.

In this passage, Jacky expresses the hope that love will save her
from the grim reality of most of the marriages she observes. She
is going to marry for love rather than simply for money –
otherwise marriage will be full of arguments. She is not being
entirely romantic about marriage – she sees the risks involved.
The only hope is that you can find someone who will understand

you and share things with you. Yet she ends up noting that love has not saved her mother – he does not help – it has turned her against him – but they must love each other. She expresses the contradiction but still clings to her belief that love will save her. This can be seen as setting up a myth that insulates her from the reality of women's position in marriage.

Another contradiction expressed in this passage is the un-acceptability of the idea of 'marrying for money'. Women's marriage role, encompassing both unpaid domestic work and the care of children within the home, weakens their already inferior position in the labour market, and renders them not only dependent on the husband's wage but also on his 'gener-osity'. It would therefore be rational for girls to think carefully about the economic implications of marrying. Yet to consider such a question would be deemed as marrying for money against the dominant code of romance. As Jacky recognizes, her mother's dependency has 'turned her against him' but this does not lead her to stress the importance of their material inequality – instead she clings to her belief that 'true love' will save her from the grim reality around, although it has not saved her mother. Subscrib-ing to the idea of love against all the odds diverts attention away from the realization of women's subordination in the marriage relationship.

It is this commitment to the myth of undemanding love which leads many girls to accept being brow beaten or physically assaulted as part of women's lot. They focus on who loves them or whom they love rather than on the way some men act. As Berthold Brecht so aptly expressed it:

He may be lame, he may be mad
He may beat her as he will
All that worries Hanna Cash, my lad,
Is – does she love him still?

In similar vein Meridel Le Sueur describes in her documentary novel of the Depression, drawn from the writings and oral narrations of women in the Workers' Alliance who met at a writers' group, how one woman said:

You know when I had that black eye and said I hit it on the cupboard. Well he did it the bastard. I don't know why I live with him, why I put up with him a minute on this earth. But listen kid, she said I'm telling you

something. She looked at me and her face was wonderful. She said
'Jesus Christ, Goddam him I love him that's why, I'm hooked like this all
my life, Goddam him I love him.'

Putting up with violence in marriage – often seen by the courts
as condoning violence – can be seen as being unable to break
away from the code of romance which demands unrequited love
'for better for worse, in sickness and in health', and whether
you're beaten black and blue to boot.

   Rather than condemning violence, as we have seen, girls instead hold the woman responsible for putting up with it, failing
to take into account the way women are often trapped financially
with children and in no position to move. Or they reduce the
problem to 'you have to be really careful who you pick'. The
question is whom to marry rather than whether to. As Sallie
Westwood points out:

When Paul Willis studied 'lads' in school they showed just how much
they wanted to leave school and rush in through the factory gates,
viewing this as the moment of choice and freedom; young women rush
out of the factory in the opposite direction into domesticity with the
same sense of a decision freely made, a choice exercised (Westwood
1984).

This research does not corroborate Westwood's view. Girls
do not rush into domesticity with quite the willingness she suggests. However, the idea that marriage is purely a question of
individual choice is ingrained and few girls are prepared to
reject the whole idea, although some seemed doubtful about the
idea of romantic love saving them:

I hate the idea of getting married because you're pregnant, or because
it's more convenient than not getting married. Getting married because
you love a bloke isn't a good enough reason. All the people I know –
including my mum – have marriages that have broken down.

For the sake of the children

Some middle-class girls reject marriage, unless it involves children, in which case it is sacrosanct:

Actual marriage, I don't think it's necessary unless you're going
to have children and I can't visualize myself having children.

Apart from that, I don't think actual marriage – a piece of paper – is all that important. I'm not religious or anything. Living in sin will do me.

Marriage I think of as with children but living together it's different, it's just two people.

If you don't want to have children it's OK to live with somebody but if you are going to have children it's better to have a stable family background. So I'd get married if I wanted children.

I'd like to marry say about 28 or 30, more that age, when you have enjoyed yourself and settled down and had a family. I would want to have a child sometime but not for a long time.

Q   Would that involve marriage?

It depends. Sometimes I don't see the need for marriage. Maybe it's for the child basically marriage. Sometimes it's security sharing a bank account sort of like that. I don't really see what difference marriage makes.

Some girls regard having children as marking 'the end of your life'.

Children – I'd like them but not for a long time. Not really until *I've sort of lived my life*. With children you've got to stay in and you can't go out much. You've got to be there to look after them. You're responsible for someone else.

I certainly want to have kids. I want to be about 30 when I have them. I want to be free from ties until then. I think by the time you're 30 you do want some thing to hold you down a bit, stop you flying around the place which I want to do as well.

I think that once you decide to have kids then you've got to accept the fact that you are gonna be tied down for a while. That's why it's important not to get married too early – until you're 28 or so. Just enjoy life when you leave school, leave college.

An interesting light on how adolescent girls construct motherhood is shown in an article by Prendergast and Prout (1980) based on interviews with 15-year-olds about what they thought life was like for mothers at home with young children. They found that most of the girls' accounts were dominated by the negative aspects of motherhood – for example, isolation, boredom, and depression. This knowledge seemed to come from the girls' observations and judgements and sometimes from their direct experience of child care. They frequently described their mothers as depressed, but seemed to accept this as something normal and to be expected if you were a mother. Yet they found a 'startling' change in direction of response between talking of their own mothers and mothers in general: 'Many girls who had given very negative descriptions (of their mothers' experiences at home) went on to agree that in fact life was good for mothers at home with young children.' Such comments as:

Most women get pleasure in looking after a child. Got someone to look after, most women have a mothering instinct and want to look after people.

What seemed to count was not their own experience but how mothers ought to feel and behave. They argue that

It can be seen that as children switch from the specificity of their own experience into that of 'mothers' a space is created around their own experiences. Filling this space is, what we would call, stereotypical knowledge. ... Their own experience did not count as knowledge in this respect ... what did count as knowledge was that which is widely available – how mothers ought to feel and behave.

The latter knowledge comes to carry the legitimacy of naturalness which, by denying the former knowledge, effectively prevents a recognition of consequent questioning of any opposition between the two.

The researchers point out that the girls' descriptions parallel the themes in Ann Oakley's study of mothers and post-natal depression (Oakley 1981). In her study, most mothers said that the whole process – the pregnancy, birth, relationship of mother and child, work of child care and social position of the mother was different from what they had expected. Four out of five said their expectations had been too 'romantic', 82 per cent said pregnancy was different from what they had envisaged, and motherhood was described by 91 per cent as contradictory to previously held images. These mothers interpreted their inability to cope and live up to the ideal as a failure to be a 'proper mother' and therefore as unnatural. This 'naturalness' of the mother's role acts to deflect concern from the burdens of child care. As Prendergast and Prout suggest, the ways that girls cope with the discrepancy between these two types of knowledge – the normative and the illegitimate – (based on their own experience) has much in common with the ways I have suggested girls reconcile the discrepancy between their knowledge of marriage and the universal expectation that that was their natural destiny. Girls push the idea of the anticipated birth of a child as far away as possible. They postpone the whole question as they postpone the idea of getting married. Sometimes they also attribute the negative descriptions of motherhood to the particular problems experienced by young mothers. As one girl describes:

It depends on the age of the mother. Older mothers are better able to cope. They're more mature. Young ones want to get about, to be free and not held down. I'd get frustrated because it's hard if you are young.

As though the isolation would go away if you were older. By attributing the trials of motherhood to the problems of young mothers, the answer or solution for them is that in the far distant future everything will be different. The question of shared child care rarely arose spontaneously but one middle-class girl when asked who would look after the children says it should be 'fifty-fifty':

I think that whoever I'm with – a boyfriend or a husband – whoever it is has got to do half of it as well. It doesn't make any difference if you're a man or a woman. You both should help in that.

Perhaps this can be seen as a glimmer of hope.

In her study of fifty-six working-class girls ages 14 to 16 from a council estate in Birmingham, Angela McRobbie (1978) found that there was wholesale endorsement of the traditional female role and of femininity simply because to the girls these seemed to be perfectly natural. McRobbie argues that two factors saved the girls from what they otherwise envisaged as an unexciting future: first, their solidarity with each other, their best-friend relationship; and second, their immersion in the ideology of romance. Although my findings confirm the importance of friendships and it is these that are the girls' major source of fun, it is not romance that saves them from an unexciting future, but having fun now before you get married. As I have shown, these girls did not talk in romantic terms although they did talk about love in relation to finding a man who will understand them, share things with them and protect them from the loneliness that they see around them. What they seem to be expressing is the rather unlikely hope that love will save them from the grim reality of most of the marriages they observe. This does not however explain why girls wholeheartedly endorse the idea that one day they will get married. Rather than explain this contradiction in terms of romanticism, one might argue that girls see marriage as the only alternative to a life of ostracism where an independent existence is an unrealistic choice not only financially (as few of them will ever be able to attract a living wage), but socially too in view of the strong constraints on the expression of any independent sexuality.

It is not only the unromantic depiction of marriage that leads me to this conclusion. It is also that girls through their relationships with boyfriends and their domestic responsibilities at home, realize that they are already having a taste of what marriage will be like.

Boyfriends

Since girls tend to look on any relationship with a boy with marriage in mind, courtship can be seen as a rehearsal for marital existence. Often the connection between now and the future is quite explicit:

The boys are sort of stereotyped men. They'd go off for evenings without the girls and go down to the pub and wouldn't expect the girls to come.

These boys were the type that bragged:

Casanovas, they've got really big heads. They're always going on about the size of their cocks – how big it is – that's the honest truth – they're always on about how big it is. Well that's what Charlie is like.

The sort of boys I don't like see girls as real conquests, and brag to their friends.

You get boys that are flash, they really act big, they think they're it.

Bossiness was often mentioned:

Boys quite often don't say what are we going to do, they sort of tell you.

He's always got to be right, all the time. I'm never allowed to be right. If I know about something and he doesn't. He's always got to be right.

Or taking girls for granted:

A boy that swears and thinks you're easy to please or he just goes round with many girls at a time.

Yeh, he goes 'Oh that's my bird, that's my bird' and then you think you're wanted. You think he loves you and then when you find out he's with someone else he says 'Oh what's the matter with you?' like this all the time and he really makes you feel as if you're going out with a real big head.

Or treating you as an object:

It's just the leers blokes give you. The leering sort of look. You know they make you feel like an object for a bloke to look at and touch . . . just for their satisfaction.

Or being possessive:

People think that it is a girl who wants to get tied down and married but it isn't true. Boys can be really possessive. The ones I go with do and you have to only go out with them and you can't go out with your friends 'cos a boy might see you and then ask you out and you might like him better. I just have to be free. When you're 15 you don't really want to get tied down or anything. But you just want to have somebody that you can feel really close to but not act as if you're married 'cos if you've got someone they say 'No, you can't do that'. It's like you're a married couple or something. And you're still sort of young and living your life, experiencing everything.

Or hitting you about a bit:

We used to talk about everything really. Just everything you talk to a mate about you could say to him . . . I know him inside out really. Every trick like y'know. He used to hit me and that – a bit of a sock but I still used to like him.

The picture girls give of boys is not completely clear cut. Several girls mention that they are attracted to boys they do not particularly like and several complain about 'sloppy boys':

Lots of girls find if you're going out with a bloke you like, he'll really treat you terrible but you'll like him more and the ones who treat you all nice and come on all sloppy about how much they love you, you really hate them. I've been in the situation where he's been saying how much he wants to marry me and it really makes me – ugh. It repulses me. One bloke I really liked he'd say he'd phone up and he'd never phone, I'd like him more for that. It's an attraction for girls if someone can't be tied down. He sort of really plays the Casanova. Everyone thinks 'Oh I'll have a go. I'll try him and tame him.'

Thus girls are attracted to boys but are aware that some boys are chauvinistic and even violent. The girls themselves are not without ambiguities in their response to this. But the overall effect is of the normality of aggressive and chauvinistic behaviour on the boy's part.

Nice boys on the other hand treat girls as friends 'who you can "talk to" and trust' (although several girls seems to think it is hard to be sure you can trust anybody). Age and intelligence are quite frequently mentioned:

I like them to be old – not old men but sort of 17 or so.

But more often trust and the way boys treat girls are the most important criteria – predictable in view of the way most boys treat girls:

I would like to be treated as just equal. I would like to treat boys the same way as I treat girls – and I like them to treat me the same as well.

Some girls explain how exciting it is to meet a boy who is fun to be with but appear surprised if they can talk to him.

He's really exciting to be with. He's so funny. He's got a really good sense of humour. Sometimes he can act like a little kid like messing about but then he's alright to be with ... you can talk to him ... I didn't expect to be able to talk to him as good as I do. I talk to him quite freely. You do get people who can't really talk to their husbands or their boyfriends.

Others were not so sure whether they wanted a boyfriend:

I don't even care, I don't even know if I want one.

None the less, the normality of chauvinism and non-communication on the part of the boys is striking. In spite of this the issue of marriage is still seen by girls as a question of finding a *nice* boy, scarce as they appear to be. One girl explains the type of boy to look out for:

> If they're kind and they chat alright and they're just kind to you. ... If he doesn't go round hitting you and punching you as some boys do nowadays ... say if he asks you out and you don't want to go with him, he slaps you or something. I don't think that's right.

Hardly an over-romantic view of the boy to seek! And the boy to avoid – a Dirty Harry:

> A boy who thinks he can touch up all the girls in the world and won't get himself into trouble and when he gets one pregnant he hides his face all the time.

Several girls thought it was from their dads that many of the boys' attributes derived. As Mandy commented:

> I think boys get a lot of their attitudes from their dads – you know if the dad comes home drunk and he beats up his wife the bloke thinks that is how life should be and he should go out and get drunk and beat up his girlfriend. I don't want to end up like my mum. I'll try and learn from the mistakes my mum has made.

Why, then, do girls get married? What I have tried to show in this chapter is, first, that the girls have a foretaste of married life through both observing and helping their mothers and through relationships with boyfriends. These experiences, by and large, do not exactly enhance the attractiveness of married life. Yet, and this is the second point I have tried to make, the various strategies pursued by the girls are essentially delaying tactics – putting off marriage till a later date, avoiding the issue by personalizing it – redefining the problem as that of finding the right man, or simply seeing marriage as inevitable either because having children requires marriage, or because being 'left on the shelf' is seen as an unacceptable alternative.

In short, few positive attractions attach to the married life as far as the girls are concerned. Yet, as far as they see it, there is just no alternative. This is what needs to be explained. What are the mechanisms which bring the girls to the view that despite the unattractiveness of marriage the question is, as one girl put it, not of *choosing* to get married or not, but whether you get married or *fail* to get married? This girl was from Diana Leonard's study (1980) in Swansea of working-class girls and boys for whom marriage was considered the only way of leaving home. A home was seen as something developed by the married couple to which there was no real notion of any alternative. To live away from home in the same town, in any other than the domestic married unit, would be seen as a real slight on one's parents. What forces this closure on all alternatives to married life is, above all, the power of the 'slag' categorization for an unattached woman who is active sexually. When we understand the way in which female sexuality is constructed and constrained by the categorization of slags and drags, how a woman's femininity and sexuality is only rendered 'safe' when confined to the bonds of marriage, we shall understand why there is just no alternative, as the girls see it, to married life.

Notwithstanding the differences in girls' experience and opportunities occasioned by class and racial stratification it is the overwhelming power of sexual categorization that steers the vast majority of girls into an acceptance of married life with its attendant forms of domination and exploitation. Once in marriage the girls will live out the very lives they had so accurately observed their mothers living and from which they had tried to insulate themselves through delaying tactics or rationalizations. They will, as Sallie Westwood vividly depicts, 'sink into his arms' and quickly 'end up in the kitchen sink' (Westwood 1984). They will learn to collude in their own oppression by insisting that management of the home and working for the family is their special preserve and that any suggestion that husbands should participate is to be contested.

To them, this was women's work, their proper work which offered them a place at the centre of family life, and through that, status and power – which work outside the home did not offer. . . .

and to take a comfort and succour from family life which will render any thought of leaving their husbands and seeking alternatives unrealistic and unrewarding.

Apart from the ideological push they receive in this direction it is quite clear that working-class women are committed to the family because it is an experience and a space which offers them some degree of autonomy over their lives and the warmth, support and affection from a group of people who matter and who in turn make a woman feel she is important and valued (Westwood 1980).

To explain women's commitment to the family in this way is to repeat the often held view that women are marginal at work because their attentions are directed elsewhere, to the sphere of the home that gives them an identity and a form of power. This research challenges this view.

Women are not 'marginal' to work because they are central to the subordinate area of the family.[4] They are marginal to work because they are discriminated against, because they are subordinate both within and outside the family, where their position is often one of oppression. As waged workers, although women now make up 40 per cent of the work force (how can that be marginal?), women are seen primarily as wives and mothers and are paid on average only two-thirds of men's earnings. Their participation in wage labour is therefore negotiated on different terms (they are only considered suitable for certain types of work, are subject to sexual harassment and are not considered serious workers) and at different rates – women earn only two-thirds of men's earnings. It is therefore only through marriage that women have access to a decent living wage.

In reality, the family can be an even greater source of inequality than the labour market, though that inequality is hidden within the privacy of the domestic economy. Jan Pahl's study (1980) of the distribution of money within the marriage relationship shows how unequal this often is, and other studies indicate that after divorce some women experience a higher standard of living on supplementary benefits than when they were married because of their lack of access to the breadwinner's wage during the marriage. Carol Smart pinpoints the extreme vulnerability of women that is

hidden much of the time by the structure of the domestic economy, particularly the institution of housekeeping which can masquerade as a wage, or simply by the privacy of domestic life that obscures the extensiveness and special nature of poverty suffered by women (Smart 1984).

It is only at the point of marriage breakdown that the poverty of women and children is revealed and women find themselves powerless to command a similar wage or salary level, and are often constricted by child-care responsibilities. Hilda Scott argues that the special poverty of women lies in the fact that their economic position depends on their relationship with a man or lack of it, and the provision he makes for them on death or divorce. This is why the recent increase in divorce in the United States has led to a feminization of poverty such that two out of three poor adults are now women (Scott 1984).

A widely accepted view, at least among men, is that 'women are out for all they can get' or, as one man I overheard recently said, 'It's always the man who draws the short straw' or, as an MP commented in the debate on the Matrimonial Clauses Bill (which has now become law), the question of 'alimony drones' who 'want a meal ticket for life' needs to be recognized. The double standard in the approach to divorce is aptly expressed by Lord Denning in the case of Wachtel and Wachtel in 1973, when he said:

When a marriage breaks up, there will henceforth be two households instead of one. The husband will have to go out to work all day and *must get some woman to look after the house* – either a wife ... or a housekeeper .... He will also have to provide maintenance for the children. The wife will not usually have so much expense. She may go out to work herself, but she will not usually employ a housekeeper. She will do most of the housework herself, perhaps with some help. Or she may remarry, in which case her new husband will provide for her.

Of course there are problems for men setting up a new family after divorce but this mainly derives from women's dependent and subordinate status both at home and in the workplace. It derives from the lack of recognition of the costs of child care and domestic labour and from the unrecognized unpaid labour which men derive from marriage. No wonder they feel they have lost out on divorce – they have often lost an unpaid servant who caters to their every need. The reality of women's subordination is rarely grasped. When Carol Smart asked magistrates in Sheffield whether they thought women divorced on low incomes should 1 be encouraged to work; 2 should receive higher welfare benefits; 3 should receive higher alimony, they disagreed with all three forms of action. Remarriage was seen as the only answer. The difficulty of managing as a one parent family was brought home to me recently in a conversation with a woman councillor who had been left widowed with two children. She had found it impossible to manage and had therefore decided to remarry though this had thrown her into depression and led to her giving up politics. It is therefore impossible to understand the lives of women without considering and analysing their relations to the domestic sphere and to the structure of sex–gender relations.

Marriage therefore is the pivotal component of a woman's experience. It is a similar experience for all women. Although it takes different forms, the unequal power relationship between the sexes is essentially the same regardless of class. For girls the experience of class is always mediated through gender. It is through marriage that girls are placed in and experience the realities of social class. Divorce, as we have seen, leads to rapid downward social mobility. Yet the inequality is denied and masked by the aura of romantic love with its connotations of a relationship between equals. The inability of boys to understand the impact of the double standard on girls' lives emerged in boys' letters I received from a teacher in Hertfordshire where an article I had written for *New Society* had been used as a focus for discussion. The boys pointed out the absence of boys from my sample and accused me of sexism. The general view was that although abuse like slag, bitch and cow were commonly used by boys, the boys held that this abuse was always used, as one boy put it, 'in a very light hearted manner'. He went on:

These words are now used so commonly (as with other much more obscene language) that they have been worn down to a point of almost meaninglessness.

This dismissal of the significance of sexual abuse is pervasive and reflects the way treating girls as sex objects and in derogatory ways is not taken seriously. Another boy commented:

When the term slag is used it is not a deep and meaningful comment on a girl's sexual behaviour but merely a general insult when nothing else comes to mind. ... This report [of my research] is pointless and proves nothing – it is an uneducated representation of how the male mind works.

He is of course right in holding that the term slag does not represent a meaningful comment on a girl's sexual behaviour, but what he fails to grasp is the constraints it places on girls and the derogation implicit in the use of the term. The way that a girl's experience is structured in a different way is not something boys can understand. It is as though in discussing class the effect of different family incomes were completely denied.

Perhaps most crucially, at the level of material economic relations sex–gender relations are at least as important as those established around the institution of wage labour and capital. Sociologists usually classify women into different class groups with reference to their husband's socio-economic class, thereby regarding economic class stratification as the only significant form of stratification. But, as Christine Delphy says, it is women's dependence on their husbands that is *itself* a form of economic stratification of equal significance (Delphy 1984). Women's dependent status is used to put women in the same social class as their husbands and then this class parity is treated as the predominant factor in the couples' relations. The crucial criterion for allocating women into a social economic class is obscured:

The relations between the man and woman within the couple, and particularly her economic dependence on him are always treated as secondary, since the shared social status – seen as more general and therefore carrying more weight in determining an individual's situation – is supposed to override internal disparities. .... Sociology uses this relationship of dependence in order to situate women within the classical system of stratification. It thus obscures the fact that women form part of another mode of production. Sociology roots its analyses in the specific antagonistic relations of production between husbands and wives and then not only denies the relationship but transforms it into its very opposite: a relationship between equals (Delphy 1984).

The different power relation between women and men goes ignored. The massive forms of labour surrounding housework and child care are simply regarded as non-work and thus outside the sphere of economic relations and stratification.

In conclusion it is worth considering the extent to which the onset of long-term youth unemployment is likely to alter this process of reconciliation to marriage and domestic labour. Paul Willis, in a series of articles in *New Society* (29 March, 5 April, 12 April 1984) emphasizes how the socialization of young people into gender roles is tied to the transition from school to work and the acquisition – by males especially – of the wage. He speculates whether 'The loss of work and the wage may have profound consequences for the traditional sense of working class masculinity.' He considers two possibilities. One is that 'Traditional male working class identity may actually be *softened* when the link with wage labour and the dignity and sacrifice of manual work is broken.' Perhaps this will be a long-term effect. But certainly the short-term effect is for young males to cope with unemployment by finding new ways to express masculinity. The loss of the acquisition of the wage leads young males to a 'gender crisis' to which one solution 'may be an aggressive asser- tion of masculinity and masculine style for its own sake' (5 April). An aggressive masculinity, combined with unemploy- ment, could well lead to an increase in the level of domestic violence faced by women. In a recent study of domestic violence Jan Pahl concludes:

Finally, it seemed that there might be an association between the violence and the unemployment of the husband. Twenty-four per cent of the men were out of work when they committed the assault which forced their wives to go to the refuge: this was at a time when the unemployment rate in Britain was around 6 per cent (Pahl 1984).

It is now over 13 per cent and for young people much higher. 40 per cent of all the registered unemployed in Britain are under 25 and just under a third have been unemployed for over a year. Female unemployment has quadrupled in the past ten years and the sex discrimination and equal pay acts have been largely ineffective. Only 11 per cent of cases taken to industrial trib- unals have been successful.[5]

This conclusion as regards young males is borne out in other research. Thus Claire Wallace in a study of unemployed young people in the Isle of Sheppey concludes:

For male youth the material and social bases of masculinity were undermined – they had no status as wage earners and no money as consumers. Consequently the *symbolic* expressions of masculinity were sometimes exaggerated. This was done in two main ways: through status enhancing gestures or activities and through the retailing of such gestures and activities later as stories. ... These stories described such things as heroic (and otherwise irrational) acts of delinquency, great orgiastic binges of drinking or drug taking, dramatic confrontations with the police, employers, the DHSS, and others in authority. As well as recounting dramatic confrontations with others such stories also tended to glorify accounts of *self* destruction and 'excessive' hedonism (Wallace 1985).

The consequences for girls could be important. If young men, in response to long-term unemployment and the absence of the wage, are beginning to seek more symbolic gestures to confirm their masculinity, then young women, it seems likely, will face no let-up in the constraints on their own behaviour in the public sphere and social life which result from the activities of boys. Indeed an increased emphasis by males on the symbolic aspects of gender relations and masculinity could lead to an intensification of the types of constraints on women which we have looked at in this study.

But unemployment has its own direct effect on the lives of girls quite apart from the behaviour of boys. For young working-class women

Unemployment may well mean a deepening of their domestic duties and their oppression. The traditional role of housewife, child carer and support may not be broken but strengthened (Willis 1984).

Wallace, also, argues that for a girl 'Lack of a job ... condemned her to the status of a junior within the home and it was more likely that she would be given domestic chores to do as well.' Tensions within the family as a result of unemployment may act as a pressure on girls to leave home and set up on their own. Often this may involve getting pregnant, getting married, or both. Thus Wallace found that:

... it was no coincidence, perhaps, that girls who had been unemployed for longer than three months out of their five years after leaving school were twice as likely to have left home, to live with a man, had children or got married than those who were regularly employed (Wallace 1985).

Girls are seen primarily as potential wives and mothers rather than waged workers. Their identities, their preoccupations and aspirations are overwhelmingly determined by their common experience of married life, of a future that they now contemplate with a cynicism based on realism and accurate perception, but to which the majority of them, within a few years, reconcile themselves.

Notes

1   Family Policy Studies Centre Fact Sheet, September 1984.
2   In the Hebrides the rate of depression was negligible, probably due to the strength of community life.
3   See Edgell, 1980.
4   The General Household Survey, *GHS 1980*, shows that in 1978, 1979 and 1980, 62 per cent of married women aged 16 to 59 years were economically active.
5   See *Sunday Times* magazine, 1 September 1985.

References

Barnard, Jessie, *The Future of Marriage*, Souvenir Press, 1973.

Brown, G. and Harris, T., *The Social Origins of Depression*, Tavistock, 1978.

Comer, Lee, *Condition of Illusion*, Feminist Books, 1974.

Delphy, Christine, *Close to Home*, Hutchinson, 1984.

Denning, Lord, Wachtel vs Wachtel, 1973, quoted in Smart, Carol, *The Ties that Bind*, Routledge and Kegan Paul, 1984.

Edgell, S., *Middle Class Couples*, Allen & Unwin, 1980.

Family Policy Studies Centre, *Fact Sheet*, 1984.

French, M., *The Women's Room*, Deutsch, 1978.

Jephcott, Pearl, *Girls Growing Up*, Faber & Faber, 1942.

Leonard, Diana, *Sex and Generation*, Tavistock, 1980.

McRobbie, Angela, 'Working class girls and the culture of femininity' in *Women Take Issue*, Hutchinson, 1978.

Oakley, Ann, *From Here to Maternity*, Penguin, 1981.

Pahl, Jan, 'Patterns of Money Management within Marriage', *Journal of Social Policy*, **9** No. 3 (1980).

Pahl, Jan, *Private Violence and Public Policy*, Routledge and Kegan Paul, 1984.

Prendergast and Prout, A., 'What will I do ... ? Teenage Girls and the Construction of Motherhood', *Sociological Review* (August 1980).

Riche, Adrienne, 'Compulsory Sexuality and Lesbian Existence', in Stimpson, C. and Person, S., *Women Sex and Sexuality*, Chicago Press, 1980.

Scott, Hilda, *Working Your Way Up To The Bottom*, Pandora, 1984.

Sharpe, Sue, *Just Like a Girl*, Penguin, 1976.

Smart, Carol, *The Ties that Bind*, Routledge and Kegan Paul, 1984.

Trenchard, L. and Warren, H., *Something to Tell You*, London Gay Teenage Group, 1984.

Wallace, Claire, 'Masculinity Femininity and Unemployment', unpublished paper presented at Sociology of Education Conference, Westhill College, Birmingham, 1985.

Westwood, Sallie, *All Day Every Day*, Pluto, 1984.

Willis, P., *Learning to Labour: How Working Class Kids Get Working Class Jobs*, Saxon House, 1977.

Willis, P., *New Society* (29 March, 5 April, 12 April 1984).

Wilson, E., *Only Halfway to Paradise*, Tavistock, 1980.

4 School

During the nineteenth century the education system was structured as much by gender as by class. Girls were educated either for domesticity or to be 'cultured wives'. The post-war institutionalization of equality of opportunity has by and large ignored gender. It has long been recognized that a major aim of educational policy should be to try and overcome the disadvantages that children carry with them from their home and class backgrounds into an educational system formally committed to equality. Latterly this concern has been extended to cover race. Thus while the influence of class background and factors surrounding race have been recognized as impediments to the equality of opportunity, gender inequalities have not been seen as obstacles at all. As late as 1963 an education system committed to formal equality was seen by the Newsom Report as a weakness from the standpoint of educating girls:

> We try to educate girls into becoming imitation men and as a result we are wasting and frustrating their qualities of womanhood at great expense to the community ... in addition to their needs as individuals our girls should be educated in terms of their main social function – which is to make for themselves, their children and their husbands a secure and comfortable home and to be mothers.[1]

It is true that in the progressive 1980s, following the Sex Discrimination Act of 1975,[2] equal opportunity policies are at least on the agenda as far as girls are concerned, even though they are far from fruition. As Jane Marshall observes:

> It was concluded that girls could now learn woodwork and boys could become a bit more domesticated. Bright girls could perhaps take sciences, competing alongside boys for high status professions. Boys could relax, take it easy, and at last do some girls' subjects without losing face (Marshall 1983).

A Department of Education survey of 1979 recognized, however, that:

> Equality of opportunity for the sexes has not in practice been easy to achieve. The choice of subjects still tends to reflect traditional sex roles with fewer girls on science courses, more girls on child development courses. In college linked courses in 4th and 5th years the boys largely select technically based studies, while the girls were mostly found taking commercial subjects such as hairdressing.

Thus the sexism of the educational system is still to a considerable extent reflected in the workings of the formal structures of the school, in for example the type of subjects that girls are pressured to choose. But as regards the formal structures of education much has changed since the last century. It is certainly no longer a question of girls being openly educated for domesticity (as described by Deirdre Beddoe in *Discovering Women's History*, the curricula of needlework, household management, cookery, laundry technique, etc.). The sexism of the curriculum is nowadays a more subtle process. But it is vitally important to understand that the educational system cannot be exhaustively described simply in terms of its formal aims and institutional practices surrounding the teaching process. Of equal importance to the formal education process is the cultural life of the school. The social process, the formation of attitudes and cultural values, the formation of groups and identities, all this is taking place as part of school life and is every bit as important as the formal education process. Indeed, as far as the location of the main dynamics of sexism and the process whereby girls take on gender specific aspirations is concerned, it may well be more important. There are two reasons why this is likely to be the case.

First, the cultural and social life of the school is not insulated from that of the family and the neighbourhood. As far as the girls (and of course boys as well) are concerned school life is an aspect, albeit a crucial one, of social life in general. The social life of the school is not divorced from the social life after school hours and at weekends in the family and the neighbourhood. Therefore the boundaries of the school as a social system are not rigidly and clearly defined. This means that the pressures towards marriage – the strong pull on girls regardless of their social class membership, towards domesticity as the main aim of life – which are daily enacted in social and family life of adolescents will also be powerfully reflected in the social life of the school. This makes the experience of school different for girls than for boys, irrespective of the commitment of teachers to formal equality.

This leads to my second point that much of what turns even the formal educational process in a sexist direction is derived from the social dynamics of the classroom. As far as girls are concerned this is associated with the classroom behaviour of boys and the response of teachers. The co-ed/single sex distinction is important for girls because what steers the formal learning process in a sexist direction often stems from the presence of boys in the classroom, and their effects on teachers' attention and time devoted to girls, sexual harassment of girls and the ability of girls to hold their own in competition with boys.

We get glimpses of the extent of boys' disruption of the classroom: their noisiness, their sexual harassment of girls, their demands for attention and their need of disciplining and their attitudes to girls as the silent or the 'faceless' bunch (Arnot 1984).

The fact that much of the pressure towards marriage and domesticity is to be found in the social life of the school rather than in the formal structure of the curriculum should not lead to the conclusion that girls end up in marriage and domestic life because they have constructed a 'counter-school culture' (as Paul Willis argued with respect to lower working-class boys) which insulates them from the formal equality and achievement orientation of the school. It is not the girls who construct sexism as a counter-culture. It is there in the social life of the school, in the presence of and the interaction with boys and in the behaviour of teachers. And of course it *is* in the formal curriculum as well. It is well known to sociologists of education that certain subjects are taught in such a way that they embody male or female role models of behaviour. Thus science and maths are taken as paradigms of truth and the advance of knowledge. They are quintessentially 'male' subjects being taught from the standpoint of the domination and the control of nature. This type of argument about the curriculum has been developed by Bourdieu and others.[3] By stressing the nature of the school as both a formal teaching structure and curriculum and *a system of social relations* between girls, between girls and boys, and with teachers, we can under-stand the variety of ways in which the girls in our study talk about school. For example, some girls are pro-school, and like going to school but are very much alienated from the teaching process. By contrast, others want to learn, are strongly oriented towards the formal teaching process but are bored and alienated from school for various reasons. A complete map of the differ-ent positions would look like the following:

Pro-school

	Academic, career oriented	Pro-school for social rather than learning activities	
Pro-learning			*Anti-learning*
	Learning oriented but alienated from school	Little interest in either learning or social activities	

Anti-school

We thus have four groups of girls, or rather four possible strate-gies that girls could be pursuing towards the school and its role in their lives, and sexism features as a factor in each strategy in a different way.

Academic and pro-school

There is a distinct group of academic and career oriented girls in the study. They are most likely to be middle-class girls in a single sex school who are minimally aware of their disadvantages by comparison with boys in the learning process. If the dynamics of those disadvantages are in any case associated with the presence of boys – for example, boys attract a disproportionate amount of teachers' time – then of course such disadvantages are minimized in a single sex school, as some feminist writers on education have recently emphasized. The differences between the attitudes of girls to school in the single sex (until recently grant aided) school compared with the mixed comprehensive are considerable. Girls attending the single sex school are on the whole far more work oriented and positive in their approach to teachers than in the other two schools. This may be partly an historical question. As Pauline Marks pointed out, the development of girls' grammar schools did embrace am emphasis on the similarity of boys' and girls' intellectual ability (Marks 1976). Intellectual accomplishments are valued more than practical ones and there is little attempt to prepare the pupils in any direct way for the role of wife and mother. In many single-sex schools the aim is to improve the position of women, unlike the education of working-class girls that is directed at domestic and traditional roles. The ethos of the school may therefore be every bit as important as whether it is single sex or mixed. At 16 the girls from the ex-grant aided school certainly seem to be more career oriented and to embrace a future that involves more than a husband and children.

I think it's important to do well at school. If you can't get a job or something, especially nowadays it's hard to get a job.

It's very liberated here but that's just because it's a girls' school. All the teachers are trying to get you out and get a good career and at another school, at a mixed school I think they're more likely to just let you do what you want. Here they think there's something wrong with you if you don't get out and get a career. They think it's great if you don't want children and you don't want to get married.

As we have seen in the previous chapter, girls at 16 do not aspire to marriage, which they view realistically, but girls from both social classes generally talk in terms of having a career.

How many of those actually go on to successful careers is an open question and the evidence suggests that many rapidly drop their high aspirations. Even girls who have excelled at 16 – and 'O' level results for girls are better than for boys – fail to go on to achieve their potential. Polly Toynbee throws some light on this question, describing how she interviewed girls who had been given every possible educational advantage, and had come from among the academically best private schools, but had chosen to go to finishing school where they were taught the most menial, badly paid work such as cooking, typing and floristry. When she asked how their families would have reacted if their brothers had dropped out after 'O' levels one girl said 'If a boy doesn't do 'A' levels, well he's a disaster isn't he? Something's wrong.' The others agreed. Polly Toynbee comments:

What occupations were their brothers destined for or already doing? Two were studying law. One was training at Kew. One was studying estate management. One was farming with his father. Others were looking to banking, business, or the city. No one said a word about carpentry, plumbing, or electrical apprenticeships – the male equivalents, perhaps, of these girls' chosen trades, in terms of low status but solid employment (*Guardian* 21.3.83).

Since all the girls protested that they wanted to work throughout their lives, Polly Toynbee asked them if they were prepared for forty years of cooking, typing and floristry, forty years in which they could look forward to very limited promotion and development of skills and talents. 'Quite frankly', said one of the girls, 'high powered women, well men just don't much like it. A man doesn't like his wife to care more about her career than about him. A job is one thing, but a top career is a bit threatening'. When asked if they wanted anything different for their daughters they agreed that they wanted girls to have the same chances as boys. When challenged for not taking up the chances already offered them one girl replied 'It's not like that, there are just things girls do and things boys do. Of course it shouldn't be like that but, frankly, that's the world we live in. You have to be very special to do something different.' Being 'very special' means being able to overcome not only the pressures towards domesticity and marriage that make themselves felt even among academically oriented girls after 16, but, for those girls who do aspire to 'a top career' the discrimination that they will face when they enter the labour market.

Academic but alienated

There are of course plenty of girls in all social classes in the mixed comprehensives who want to learn and do want careers. Some fantasize about careers in order to delay thinking about marriage and it is not until after 'O' level that girls as a group fall behind boys[4] as they reconcile themselves to the reality of marriage and poor opportunities. But they do not have to do this by developing a subculture in opposition to the school, like Willis's lads, because at school teachers' attitudes, subtle pressures as regards subject choice, parental pressure, poor career opportunities and – in mixed schools – the attitudes and behaviour of boys, all combine to push them in this direction. The enthusiasm of such girls for a career is quite striking:

I want to learn more now, I don't just want to work in Woolworths. I mean even if I do get my exams I don't want to do something like work in a shop . . . I want to do something that I like doing.

I think I'm just as capable, or more capable than a lot of boys. I know I could get a good job and it annoys me when they start immediately presuming just because you're a girl, you know, they're going to be the ones who go out to work and you're going to be the ones to stay at home, even if you're more intelligent than them.

Gita, an Asian girl, sees attractiveness as important for a career:

I wish I had a nice figure, especially for my career I wish I had a better body. I think I'm too skinny.

Again, it was the middle-class girls who stood most chance of achieving a career.

There might be one or two working class girls doing 'O's but generally they're the ones doing CSEs. I mean, there are some middle class girls doing CSEs but there's more of them than working class doing 'O' levels.

There was a degree of fantasy about career, motivated by escape or postponement of the inevitability of marriage. But quite irrespective of class one finds many more girls in the mixed schools who want to learn and who want careers but are alienated from the school.[5] Three things serve to alienate them from the school. One is the presence of large numbers of other girls who have already abandoned the orientation to career and work.

There are only three in the class who want to work. We can't work properly though, 'cos they just mess around and we try to do some work but then they just come up to us and make a lot of noise so that you can't work. One day the teacher was trying to teach us and they suddenly came into the class room. They started crowding around our desks singing stuff like that, being really stupid. You can't go and tell the teacher and tell on them 'cos then they start picking on you even more and saying that you need a teacher to help you and all that. Even if you tell them to shut up, they start on you even more.

Another girl says:

School, I know I have to come and it's good for me. I want to learn
and get a good job but I don't like working, I find it boring. We throw
things at each other or shout all the time or argue. It makes school life a
bit less boring. You say 'Oh, I'm going to work' then it's the same thing
all over again you get bored.

Here the problem is less the presence of others who don't want
to work than the fact that lessons are boring. Many of the girls
associated this with the attitude of the teachers which girls most
often mentioned as alienating them from school. Some teachers
are overtly sexist:

This jewellery teacher. He thinks the woman is just there for the home
and nothing else. We often have arguments with him. We say women
should have equal rights to men and he says 'not really – you don't *have*
to say yes when we ask you to marry us'. It's because girls have been
brought up to think they should do lots of work and the boys are
expecting us girls to do all the work. They expect their mums to do it
and when they marry they expect the girls to do it.

A black working-class girl speaks bitterly about the sexism she
has received from a teacher:

He picks me out. 'Jenny', he goes. I go 'Yeah'. You little 'f_____'.
'What right have you to call me a fucker?' I goes. 'What right have you
to insult me?' He goes 'What?' I was gonna kill him – if no teacher had
come in that door, I swear it, I was really gonna beat him. I hate
teachers like that. He's heard from another teacher that I'm cheeky so
he goes 'Oh Jenny, cheeky little cunt, ain't you' ... I can't stand people
swearing at me.

Of course not all teachers are like this:

Some teachers treat girls and boys the same. But it depends on what the
teacher's like. Some of them think girls should do this and that, and
some of them think they should be treated the same.

Examples of recognized sexual stereotyping by teachers are rare
in the schools we looked at. Often of course the girls would not
notice it. Rather what alienates them from teachers is the lack of
seriousness and commitment that they often identify in teachers.

Differences in the quality of pupil–teacher relationships and styles of interaction are described by the girls in our study and often given as a reason for failing to choose a particular subject. A common criticism of teachers is their failure or unwillingness to explain what girls do not understand, often resulting in what John Holt describes as 'learning to fail' (Holt 1964).

The girls' evaluation of the teachers indicates an awareness of the education system and what it could offer. Where girls do not like a teacher or are 'turned off' by teachers it is, in many cases, less that girls have developed some other sub-cultural orientations (like Willis's lads) than that the teachers are not treating them sensitively. Girls like teachers who stimulate their interest and can keep order. Teachers that are disliked are either bossy and authoritarian or try to be chummy and ignore the status differences between themselves and girls in an artificial way which only provokes the contempt of the latter. Teachers are liked if they are:

not so much strict but assert their authority. We're often talking about it. You like teachers who can say what they want and get their homework in on time.

She doesn't just tell you to do that and leave you. She'll see if you can do it and if you can't she'll sit there until you've learned.

Or:

A teacher who makes us do the work but is still nice while she's at it. Not really strict but doesn't get all chummy with us.

These girls, therefore, want to learn. They are alienated from the school by bossy and authoritarian or overfriendly teachers who, the girls feel, prevent them from learning:

Q   What sort of teachers do you dislike?

The bitchy ones that make remarks about you and things like that. Like in certain lessons I just don't want to work 'cos she always says to me 'You're always mucking around and don't try.' So I just give up and muck around.

The ones that treat us like babies and are sarcastic with everyone. The way they look us up and down as if we're shit.

Likewise, overfriendliness on the part of the teachers was frequently seen as covering up for lack of seriousness about learning:

Q   What teachers don't you like?

The ones who can't be bothered. Over friendly and just try to be really chummy with you. . . . They interfere if you look depressed. They'd come and say 'What's the matter with you then, is it at school or at home?' I'd rather tell my friends a thing like that.

Another girl is very articulate:

I hate the teachers in this school, can't stand them, to me they're not teachers. When I first came to this school we had teachers who dressed up as if they was a teacher, y'know what I mean, like three-piece suit, tie, you know, they were strict. And the thing that made you learn in class was that you were afraid of them. If you didn't do your work you thought he's gonna hit me or put me in detention. Through that you used to learn, you used to work. But now the teachers are like the kids. I swear this is no joke. A teacher goes to me 'you gotta fag?' I goes 'no'. He goes 'Why not? I would give you one.' I goes, 'I wouldn't ask you for one.' I wouldn't dare ask a teacher if he'd got a fag. In school, you know, a teacher goes to me 'have you gotta fag?' two days ago . . . before you know it all the teachers are going to go 'gotta fag? gotta fag?' because they know if I'd given one teacher one. I think teachers shouldn't do that. They should try and stop us from smoking but they do it themselves.

This is not to say that teachers are not liked for being open. On the contrary, as Brenda says:

I like a teacher who is open. She'll say 'Oh I've got to go home tonight and do this.' She can talk to us.

The third factor that alienates girls from school and learning is the behaviour of the boys. Obviously this is not a factor in the single sex school but it is important in the mixed ones.

Well I think boys of that age, they're sort of putting you off and . . . you get people who are really influenced by the boys' presence. Some people just can't concentrate. You're always looking at the person behind you or around the corner who's flicking his pencil or talking to you or something.

Boys often speak disparagingly to girls and as in this example use the same sexist language in normal social interchange:

If he wants to borrow a ruler or something and we don't give it to him
'cos we borrowed him something before, and he like calls you a pratt.
He says 'All right pratt. You're so damned tight you won't give us
anything.' So we go 'That's right.' Then every time he comes to the
lesson they call you 'pratt' 'pratt' every time you do something even if
you go up and ask the teacher something, 'Pratt's sitting down on the
chair', 'Pratt's got a ruler' and all the rest of it. You don't have a chance.

In the mixed schools girls are often aware that they get less than
what they consider to be their fair share of teacher attention.
Several girls in a group discussion mention this:

Girls get much less attention than boys 'cos boys make a fuss and make
themselves noticed – they wanna be noticed so they make a racket.

They think they're it.

If we open our mouths we get into trouble but the boys don't 'cos
they're harder than us.

Boys can take teachers down a peg or two but with the girls they can
shout at us as much as they like and we won't say nothing. We think 'Oh
it's my fault. I should have done this', but with the boys they say 'Oh
you've been messing around, just watch it.'

An example of the way girls are pushed off using school equip-
ment is described in a group discussion about a table tennis craze
at one of the schools:

Boys go around in groups, most of them play table tennis, play it night
and day, play it at breaktime, 20 minutes, then at dinner time for an
hour. They do it all the time, it's amazing.

Q   The girls don't join in?

When it first started they used to. We had two tables then, and had a
group per table but then the boys said 'You have to join in with us if you
want to play.' A couple of girls did but I never did as I'm not in love with
table tennis.

The girls went on to describe what they thought of the girls who
insisted on playing.

The couple of girls who did were just doing it for attraction. It's like
saying 'I'm big.'

Q   What did you think of them?

Well me and my mate call them show-offs.

The question of teachers paying more attention to boys than girls has been the subject of some interesting research. Dale Spender in *Invisible Women* reported how when she taped classes she was teaching and had felt that she was giving equal attention to boys and to girls she found in fact that

the maximum time I spent interacting with the girls was 42% ... and the minimum with the boys was 58%. It is nothing short of a substantial shock to appreciate the discrepancy between what I *thought* I was doing and what I actually *was* doing.

Girls are also aware that undisciplined behaviour will have different results for them than for boys:

If they got told off by a teacher boys just say 'Yeh Yeh' like that and they go and hit the teacher. If we hit the teacher we'd be sent straight out of school for good. They just get sent home for a couple of days and then brought back.

Such, then, are the obstacles that face girls who want to learn but are put off by the obstructions they find in their way – particularly the behaviour of boys and teachers – and end up feeling alienated from the school even though they are not alienated from learning as such. But many of the girls are very much alienated from the learning process. They often like school but if they do so it is for social rather than educational reasons, as a place to meet their friends, and boys. Other girls, by contrast, just cannot wait to leave.

Pro-school, anti-work

Some girls are not interested in work but still value school life as a form of contact with friends. As Janey says: 'What makes school fun is seeing your mates.' And Maureen:

There're a lot of groups that are work oriented. I'm in the same group as my friends because I suppose we're the same sort of ability. And all the others are the same as their friends. You're more influenced by your friends, like to work or not to work, then you're gonna be in the same group as them. . . . You're very influenced by that, I think. I was saying that, but I'm not very much like it 'cos my friends all go home and swot up for exams but I'm pretty lazy, I just can't be bothered to do it. I think it's because I don't like school, and they don't press me now.

Anti-school, anti-work

The group most alienated from school are those girls who rejected both the learning process and any orientation to a career and at the same time do not focus their lives around school as a social environment. Most of these girls cannot wait to leave, get a job, and in many cases are already heavily socialized into domestic labour and housework routines. This girl has no positive thoughts about school:

When you're out of school it's really good, it's so funny, nothing boring ever happens. It's just good . . . when you're in school it's just horrible.

Another girl says:

The one thing I really don't like about school is there's a lot of apathy. People are really apathetic. They just haven't got the energy to do anything. They just sit around, can't be bothered.

It is these girls that are in the process of insulating themselves from the whole world of career and achievement. As Sarah Delamont has pointed out:

There is a sense in which we know why many working class boys reject school, even if we do not know what, if anything, can be done about it. We do not know why working class girls who are more favourable to school, continue to opt for leaving without any qualifications that will support them economically. Boys such as those studied by Willis seem to have a realistic perception of their future while girls who are their equivalent do not seem to realise that they will have to work for most of their lives in badly paid, unskilled jobs unless they leave school with qualifications, even if they marry. Adolescent girls seem blinded to the realities of the labour market by the rosy glow of romance, in ways that boys are not, and schools seem to be failing to dispel that rosy glow (Delamont 1980).

As I have argued in other chapters, it is less the 'rosy glow' of romance' than the realism concerning the inevitability of marriage. As we have seen also in other chapters the fantasizing of the future is one way of dealing with this. Such optimism or unthought out 'career' aspirations are so often the other side of the coin of a realism about the actual future. This girl is not really clear *what* she is going to do and consequently oscillates between the mundane and the fantasy of travel:

I'm hoping to work in a shop 'cos I do a Saturday job there so I'll probably see if I can stay on there. Then I want to save up and go to the States. I don't think anyone would stay in this country when they're young. You'd probably end up getting engaged and I don't want the bother ... or I'd work in a pub – people in pubs are happy ain't they? I want to work somewhere where people are lively, not dull.

But many of the girls have already abandoned the idea:

I'm going to leave next year. I'm not staying on, I think it's a waste.

Q   What are you going to do when you leave school?

I dunno. I want to be a kennel maid. I just love dogs.

Others are more realistic. Jacky, when asked what she sees herself doing in five years' time, replies:

In five years' time. Right, so I'm 21 right? I see myself pushing a pram. I don't see myself working actually. Either at home or queuing at the Labour Exchange, something like that. ... By the time I'm a bit older, out of every hundred girls in every year at school, by the time they reach the third year twenty out of a hundred are pregnant. A girl in my class she's got a baby who's a couple of months old. I don't see myself working.

Many of the girls are already participating in their future roles of domestic labour – to the detriment of their school work – by helping mother with housework. The amount of time spent on housework is compatible with McRobbie's finding that 14–16-year-olds attending a youth club spent between fourteen and sixteen hours a week on domestic work and were not joined in this work by their brothers (McRobbie 1978). Again, there are class differences. The amount of domestic work you do depends on your parents' attitude to schooling and career. A middle-class girl puts it like this:

It's got to do with your parents, your background, your upbringing. 'Cos if you mix with different people their mums and dads treat school in a completely different way.

Q   Can you give an example of the difference?

I think maybe say if you take a day off school or something some of their mums like them to take a day off to help them, but my mum wouldn't.

Frequently, girls who do domestic work complain that it interferes with their homework, although they seem to think it reasonable for their mums to ask for some help.

I don't mind 'cos my mum can't do it all herself. I've got my homework to do and half the time I don't do it. You wanna do your homework and you wanna help your mum, like you're sitting down doing your homework and your mum says 'Josie, can you do a job for me?'

The amount of help varies considerably. Some of the girls report a heavy load, especially if the mother is houseproud.

My mum is very houseproud ... I do three jobs a week and I dry up every night. Like yesterday I went to the baths and done three hours washing ... well at least from 5pm to 7pm and I ironed it all for her, I did an hour and a half's ironing. Day before, I did out the bedroom, cleaned the bath and made my bed. It's my mum, she's so clean you can't drop a crumb.

Sheila said she does forty-four hours a week housework:

On Saturday I spend most of the day – 5–6 hours a day I help my mum and the days at the weekend and on Sunday I don't go out at all. I'm indoors helping to clean up the place so it's about forty-four hours altogether.

And she even takes her mum's paid job:

It takes me just over an hour at night and I get £1.50 a night for it. ... It's supposed to be my mum's job but she gives it to me. They don't know 'cos I'm too young.

The National Child Development Study (Fogelman 1978) found half the sample of 12,000 16-year-olds surveyed worked in term time, though the number of hours worked varied. When this is added to their domestic responsibilities it adds up to no mean sum.

What determines which of these four courses are taken by girls through the education system? Obviously the type of school has an influence. Girls in the single sex school are most career oriented and the presence of boys as a disturbing factor does not apply. We have seen that class is also important. Middle-class girls are more likely to be career oriented and working-class girls more likely to be already involved in domestic chores at the expense of school and homework. The girls are very conscious of class as manifested by accent and life style. A middle-class girl says:

I think there's too much class. Everyone's sort of classed as 'Oh we're snobs.' They always think of us as snobs. Very much your accent I think. I mean, there's one girl in our class who everyone looks down on (and) says 'God, she's horrible.' She's got a strong upper-class accent. Then there're a lot of girls in our class who are East End and everything. They think of us as the brainy ones. The others are the CSEs.

Class divisions in behaviour and leisure time activities are reproduced in the school:

When we arrived at this school the middle class were doing the same thing as the other middle class and the lower class as the other lower class. The middle class go out to classical concerts with their parents. You have to make friends from where your own interests are and when you're young your interests are what your parents' interests are so they sort of depend on class 'cos you sort of go along with your parents.

Working-class girls are aware that they would never participate in the same milieu:

They [the middle-class girls] talk and dress and act older than they are. They care about their image. They've got a much better social life, always going to concerts and parties. My social life is rubbish, not very good at all.

Another working-class girl says:

I never get to meet new people. I meet a few but very few. I don't go to parties, I don't even know about any. I went to a youth club but it was really dead and the people there were kids. I just didn't bother going out any more.

One reason for working-class girls leading more socially re-stricted lives is of course financial. As Mandy, a working-class girl, explains:

My friends they have to face that one week they have no pocket money so they aren't able to do something whereas the others can always sponge money if they want it. They never have to say 'Well I've got no money. I can't go somewhere,' whereas we say 'Oh I'm skint this week.' or 'It's my week for being poor this week.' Then the next week you'll buy her a coffee or something – they [the middle-class girls] don't seem to be like that. I think some girls are very over protected.

Some girls considered that class differences stood out more in school than outside:

I think the class thing is, like, more in schools, because, like, outside school I've got friends who are completely working class, upper class and mixed. But in school – it's probably the same in most institutions – you club up, go together with your own class.

In 1970 Ronald King researched the impact of class and gender on educational achievement in state schools and reported that middle-class boys were the most advantaged and working-class girls the most disadvantaged, the former having twenty-one times more chance of taking a full-time degree course than the latter. He discovered that the class gap (ratio of middle class to working class) rose as the educational level rose. At each educational level the sex gap increased (King 1981).

But irrespective of class there is the overpowering pressure of gender stereotypes which act on all girls. The weight of all the pressures we have looked at throughout this study affects the girls' performance at school. The ever-present power of the 'slag' category is not restricted to girls' social life *as opposed to* their educational performance. As I have argued, the school is both a set of social relations and a formal educational process. But the two aspects, it is worth emphasizing again, do not just exist side by side, they are in interaction: the social dynamics of the classroom and the playground influence the aspirations and performance of pupils in the formal learning situation. The aspects of the control of girls through 'slag' that we have looked at in other chapters thus have a crucial bearing on actual educational performance. Mandy Llewellyn points out that 'what happens to girls is determined within certain boundaries by the very fact of their being girls and not by their being pupils or working class or academically successful.' She points out that the categories girls place each other in are influenced by notions of appropriate gender behaviour. In one of her examples she shows how a girl who was ostracized for academic failure was also seen as a bad girl in that she engaged in non-appropriate feminine behaviour such as taking the lead in social interaction with boys. This of course is confirmed in the analysis of the power of the slag label in this study, but an aspect of equal importance to be considered is the extent to which appropriate feminine behaviour (bounded by the threat of being labelled a slag) itself places girls at a disadvantage as regards academic orientation and achievement. Some of the girls in Mandy Llewellyn's study talked about girls who wanted a career very much in the same way as we have seen girls talk about one another as slags throughout this study:

Likewise the non-exam girls perceived the top-stream girls as 'clever', 'snotty', 'keenos', 'stuck up', but also: 'Exams won't get them nowhere, they'll be out with their prams next year – if anyone'll have 'em.' 'You see the way they dress? – wouldn't be seen dead like that.' 'Taint never seen them with a lad' (Llewellyn 1980).

The slag/drag dichotomy or the too tight/too loose distinction is one that is used by different groups of girls against each other. As Jacky says:

In class, in school – people are always calling you a slut – you're either a tramp or a snob.

When asked why girls from different class groups did not mix she says:

It's probably 'cos we think that they look down on us and they probably think that we look down on them, you just assume this is what happens and the minute you see them, a wall builds up and you don't want to break it. You just accept it.

One is reminded of the reaction of Christine Keeler (the call girl whose affair with Jack Profumo, Foreign Secretary in the early 1960s, led to his resignation) to her ghost-written autobiography where she expressed concern at being called a 'scrubber' rather than a 'tart'. Asked whether the book accurately reflected what she thought and how she felt, she replied:

It got me right, it has got me emotionally right. There's one word I don't like in the passage 'ruining my life may not seem important to some, considering what I was, just a pretty scrubber ...'. I wanted to change it to 'tart'. 'Scrubber' implies someone who can't talk properly and wears horrible clothes but I always had a bit of class to me. I'm sure Jack Profumo wouldn't have gone out with a scrubber. Perhaps they should have written 'just a pretty nobody'.

Class combines with sexism as depicting the 'loose' woman as dirty, badly dressed and a 'scrubber'. As we have seen, some girls describe a 'slag' as of low intelligence or dishevelled and untidy. Similarly, the label 'slut' often carries the connotation of lower working classness with it. Irene Payne describes a working-class girl's experiences in a middle-class, single sex grammar school:

The uniform couldn't have been better designed to disguise any hints of adolescent sexuality. I suppose that shirt and tie, the 'sensible' shoes, thick socks and navy blue knickers were part of a 'more masculined' image. It was as though femininity had to be sacrificed to the pursuit of knowledge. ... Ideas about dress were based on notions of 'nice' girls and not so nice girls with both class and sexual connotations (Payne 1980).

In similar fashion, as we shall see in the next section, the sexist category of slag is part of the raw material out of which racist views are elaborated.

Girls and race

At school there is little evidence of a strong personal racism on the part of white girls towards black girls of West Indian origin:

The girls in school don't hang around in one group of coloureds, they sort of mix, they chip in. We've got one coloured girl and three white girls in my group and everyone gets on well together.

Some of the white, mainly middle-class, girls will challenge racism when they come across it in their friends:

The other day it was a friend of ours got in an argument with a girl who had her cousin beaten up by coloured people and she said that she just can't stand coloured people and we said you should hate the people who did it but not just because of the colour of their skin or whatever. And she was really anti-coloured from them on.

Trouble involving race was occasionally mentioned, as by Tina, a white working-class girl from South London:

There's a lot of trouble at our school, a lot of argument.

Q   What was the trouble about?

It involved a lot of black girls, near enough all the black girls in our school. There were lots of them that when you were walking home there was a big group, about fifty, of them walking behind you which was scary.

But it was predominantly outside the school where the girls became more conscious of racial difference:

Q   You said that black girls call white girls slag and vice versa. Do you mix with black girls?

At school they're alright. They mix in as if they were the same colour. They don't look different. But in the flats they are all wearing modern clothes and they're all older. They take pride in their clothes. They wear white and look nice.

It is to be expected that the awareness of difference should focus on dress because:

It's very important what you wear 'cos you sort of label a girl by the clothes she's got on.

The awareness of dress differences then becomes a key theme in the feelings of racial antagonism between black and white girls in the public spaces outside the classroom. Jane, a white girl, describes how it is black girls she is most frightened of when she goes out and that if you dress like some black girls – wearing brightly coloured cotton – then you are 'asking for it'.

Then we went to the Lyceum, all of us looked really smart and there was this group of black girls and they were all going 'Tchch' and looking us up and down and you feel so uneasy with them.

Black girls also feel themselves on the receiving end of innuendo concerning dress, from white girls. Wilma complains about the way

they tease you about the way you dress, sometimes the way you walk. . . . They [the white girls] think they're perfect. That's why. They say something to you and when you say it back they say 'what did you say it about me for?' They don't like it. They can say it to you but you can't say it to them.

This is echoed by Sharan:

Some of them [white girls] are all trendy, the sort of dresses and that, and then there're some of them that are really bitchy. The thing that gets me is they take the piss out of our clothes and then half of their clothes come from jumble sales. I couldn't get my clothes from a jumble sale.

This bitching about clothes is of course no different from relations between girls in terms of subcultural styles. A white girl talks about trendies in much the same way:

They might not mean any harm, they might not be that bad, as bad as they look, but their appearance makes them stand out and that's what makes them look weird and you think 'God I can imagine her' . . . straightway she gets a bad reputation even though she might be decent inside.

What this illustrates is not that racism is 'just another' form of bitching between girls over dress and style of behaviour, but rather that racism constructs its stereotypes out of the content of everyday interpersonal interaction. The processes by which girls are labelled as slags, irrespective of race, become one component of the way in which racial stereotypes are constructed and perpetuated. The category of slag and slut is part of the raw material out of which racist views are elaborated. There are two reasons for this. First, racist and sexist stereotypes operate in ways which, although not identical, are in some respects similar. I have already argued that there is a vacuousness and ambiguity about the term slag which detaches it from any particular characteristics of a girl's behaviour and thereby enables it to function as a general mechanism of control of girls' sexuality. Racial stereotypes operate, as Allport explained, in a way which has some analogies:

There is a common mental device that permits people to hold to prejudgements even in the face of much contradictory evidence. It is the device of admitting exceptions 'There are nice Negroes but ...' or 'some of my best friends are Jews but ...'. This is a disarming device. By excluding a few favoured cases, the negative rubric is kept intact for all other cases. In short, contrary evidence is not admitted and allowed to modify the generalisation; rather it is perfunctorily acknowledged but excluded (Allport, 1954, p.23).

This process of acknowledging and then excluding exceptions is illustrated by this snippet of conversation where Karen elaborates on the racial prejudices of herself and her friends:

Like me ... Carol and me and Susan .... And we was talking about what people, like we were sat in these flats talking talking and I just said ... A Paki come along and Pam says 'Oh I hate Pakis' and I go 'Oh I hate the Jews' and Susan goes 'I hate black people'. And I goes 'How can you hate black people, Sybil's black?' And like Susan and Pamela and me were all white and she goes 'I don't really' ... she goes 'I hate golliwogs', that was it, she didn't say blacks y'know. And I says 'What do you mean you hate golliwogs? My best friend's black'. And she goes 'Yeah, so's mine.' So I goes 'Yeah? So how can you hate them?' And she goes 'Oh I don't hate all, I just hate some of them.' And Pamela goes, 'I hate all Pakis' and we just started talking about the Jews and Pakis and like she just told me she hated Pakis ... no reason, she just hates them. I hate Jews for a reason.

Karen's reason for hating Jews is that

A Jew knocked my dog down and he died, so ever since then I've hated Jews and I hate all Jews.

Q   You think all Jews are like that?

Yeah now. Only them that wear the black thing and that and ... I had a Jewish friend and I didn't know she was Jewish and I was watching Jesus of Nazareth up her house one day and I said to her when the Jews come on, I said 'Oh look, the Jews' and she said 'I'm Jewish' and her dad

was there and all and she goes her dad's Jewish – he's not one of them Jews
that wear the black thing. .... Ever since then I don't play with her.

Q   Do you like her or not?

No not a lot. That weren't the only reason I didn't like her. There were
other reasons but that made it worse.

Karen's incoherence illustrates both sides of the process that
Allport was describing. On the one hand a counterfactual example to a racist generalization will be happily incorporated
without disturbing the generalization. And on the other hand a
single instance will be held up as a sufficient reason for subscrib-
ing to a generalization about an ethnic or religious group.

Thus both the slag categorization and racist categorization are
forms of labelling that are difficult to pin down to any hard
specific content which could be shown to be untrue and lead to
the withdrawal of the label. For slag, this is because of the
ambiguous way in which it is used, and in the case of race by
refusing to allow any exceptions to modify the basic racist stereotype (Allport called this 're-fencing'). It is thus easy to see how
slag can come to fulfil the requirements of racism. Racial stereotyping of blacks by whites and of whites by blacks occurs among
the girls through the familiar devices of slag and bitching which
are at the same time being used by both girls and boys in a way
which ends up constraining the freedom of girls irrespective of
racial group.

In a Guardian article (5 September 1985) on racism in the
London borough of Redbridge, David Rose describes how racial
and sexual abuse are often combined. A 19-year-old Asian girl
Sunjita describes what happens:

If I'm with a white boy, say just on the way home from college. they
shout in the street 'What's it like to fuck a Paki?' or if I'm on my own
with other girls it's 'Here comes the Paki whore, come and fuck us Paki
whores, we've heard you're really horny.' Or maybe they'll put it the
other way round, saying that I'm dirty, that no one could possibly want
to go to bed with a Paki. .... I don't think any white person can possibly
identify with what it's like.

But it is not just that slag is a label that has a fluidity similar to
racist stereotypes. There is a crucial sexual dimension and content at the root of racism which leads it to absorb and work

through sexist categories. Even though others with a similar fluidity may be available, and used – intelligence for example – sexual behaviour has been a foundation stone of racist mythology in western societies. In *Black Women in White America* Gerda Lerner explains the centrality of sexual mythology concerning black women:

By assuming a different level of sexuality for all blacks than that of whites and mystifying their greater sexual potency, the black woman could be made to personify sexual freedom and abandon. A myth was created that all black women were eager for sexual exploits, voluntarily 'loose' in their morals, and therefore deserved none of the consideration and respect granted white women. Every black woman was, by definition, a slut according to this racist mythology; therefore to assault her and exploit her sexually was not reprehensible and carried with it none of the normal sanctions against such behaviour. A wide range of practices reinforced this myth ... the taboos against respectable social mixing of the races ... the different legal sanctions against rape, abuse of minors and other sex crimes when committed against white or black women (quoted in Bell Hooks 1981, p. 59).

This 'animal' sexual appetite and behaviour of the black woman finds a reflection in a comment by a white girl in our study:

They look black and somehow stronger. If you got a white girl and a black girl you say 'Oh she looks stronger *'cos she's black'* (italics added).

Racism, of course, involves more than interpersonal stereotypes. The relations between girls are not the only terrain on which the massive institutional racism of British society makes its impact. Treatment by police, the denial of job opportunities, treatment by teachers, lie alongside the relationships between the girls:

Q   Do you get much racism in school?

Not really. Girls don't show it a lot really but the teachers are.

However, Alice (white) does think that relations with black girls are influenced by the latters' anticipation of and experience of institutional discrimination.

In school we get on with them but on the outside we don't 'cos they think we're rotten just 'cos you're white, and they think when we grow up we're going to be police and bullies so they think 'why don't we pick on them first'. They get their own back 'cos of the police and we get into trouble for it. If we go to the police they start calling us favourites.

How far have girls' attitudes changed?

Two of the schools where we interviewed girls were attempting to combat gender discrimination – one with a girls only maths group and both with discussions about sexism. In this last section I shall look at some of the girls' views about women's liberation and the way girls cope with sexism from boys. As we have seen, some changes have occurred.

Sex outside marriage, as long as it is confined to a steady boyfriend, preferably with engagement and marriage in mind, is acceptable. Girls are more career oriented and almost all the girls envisaged work as an important if secondary part of their lives.[6] It is evident that social class differences do exist and the middle-class girls are more likely to be critical of chauvinism and the double standard. As one sexually experienced, very mature girl about to start an 'A' level course in science says:

Some girls have different attitudes. The girls who are thinking of getting engaged already are the girls who talk about sluts and talk about people who sleep around and really look down on them. And the boys that they know wouldn't touch them with a bargepole but it doesn't really involve my sort of circle. I suppose that's more about being liberated. The boys who go down the pub are the sort who sneer at girls who sleep around. But the sort who talk to girls as friends and take them down to the pub and sort of have a good night out with the girls and the boys together not really thinking about what sex they are, they're the sort ... they take it more lightly and if they can sleep around why shouldn't the girls. They're more likely to think of it like that. Which is really only fair. 'Cos you don't get girls who say 'Oh that boy's a real whore, don't go near him, he's dirt.'

Other girls agreed that the double standard of sexual morality is weakening:

There's all this nastiness about – a man who sleeps around is just a man who sleeps around and a woman who sleeps around is a real slag and you've got to keep away from her. But I think in my circles that sort of thing is fading away. Obviously, things like that are fading away more and more over the years. People are out for more sexual equality. Although boys will probably want more sex than girls but I don't see any reason why they [girls] shouldn't have sex. It's not all that much of a big step really.

Girls who express such views are unusual and for most working-class girls, even those who are aware of the double standard (and by no means all girls were), to resist the categorization is difficult, as the label attacks girls individually and it is as individuals that they are left to resist. Humour is a common method of dealing with abuse. As one girl explains:

Sometimes I go in the toilets and I see my name written up 'Ann's a slag' or something like that. I just laugh like if someone come up to my face and told me I was a slag or a slut I'd just laugh. So long as you're not one then you've got nothing to worry about.

The irony is that it is always difficult to prove that you are not a slag and the label bites.

Putting down boys is another tactic. When I was interviewed on the Jimmy Young show I was asked how girls respond to sexual abuse, as my interviewer said he 'had never met a girl who did not give as good as she got and could not stick up for herself'. The implication here is that any girl worth her salt can cope with the double standard. To do so in any other terms than to deny the accusation is to come up against the whole weight of taken-for-granted sexual morality. Other girls are aware of how unfair the double standard is, but are resigned to living with it:

Boys can sleep around and aren't called anything, but girls who do are called slags.

Q   What do you think about that?

I think it's unfair discrimination – but that's the way it goes. We all think it's unfair but somehow it just happens like that.

Wendy does describe how some girls adopt the stance of boys bragging to take the micky out of more conventional girls:

They brag about who they've got off with, who they want to get off with and things like that. *It's just out of order.* But they do, they come to you and say 'Guess who I've ...' y'know ... I mean, we didn't know her. She was like trendy and had her own mates. She just come round, ponced a fag or something. Then just turned round and said that to us. We didn't want to know about it.

Wendy strongly disapproves of this:

> I mean, say someone would tell their own little group but this girl
> – she told us – we hadn't got nothing to do with her. Just showing
> off.

This response is a far cry from the accolades that would fall on a
boy who announced his conquests, nor could you imagine a
group of girls sharing their sexual adventures when a boy is
present. Occasionally girls mention collective ways of dealing
with sexual harassment which are more successful, like this incident in the changing rooms:

> The boys love coming into the girls' changing rooms when they're
> changing. This boy right, we made a decision next time he comes in,
> grab hold of him and start taking his clothes off and see how he feels.
> All the girls were watching him. He never came back.

Part of the difficulty in retaliating successfully is that there is no
vocabulary of abuse against a boy. As Anna describes:

> If a girl sleeps with two different people then she's considered a slag but
> if a boy does it's good. I think it's really bad. It really annoys me. I call
> boys tarts.

The problem is that to call a boy a tart has no cultural meaning
so makes no impact.

  Although other girls contest the unfairness, laugh abuse off or
even boast about their sexual exploits to girls – but obviously not
to boys – for a joke, no girl is immune from the disapproval of
publicly admitted sex. All girls agree:

> It is really awful when you get a reputation and it's really hard to get rid
> of a reputation even if you get to be really good.

In view of this girls might be expected to support the aims of
women's liberation to fight against the subordinate position of
girls and women and the derogatory way girls are treated. Far
from it. The image of the women's libber as depicted in press
reports and stereotypes of unfeminine women attracts little sym-
pathy from most girls. Take these comments:

Like stereotyped women. Women who are completely anti men. . . .

Anti men . . . like women on top.

I know this sounds as if I'm anti women's lib but at the moment I think it used to be the man that had the job and the woman who stayed at home and I think it should be like a medium where whichever one wants to go out apart from at the birth of a child when the woman's the only one who can look after it, but at the rate it's going it'll be the woman who is kicked out whether she likes it or not.

Most girls seem to find the views of Women's Liberation very extreme though there is no evidence that feminism has developed in the way they fear. Ideas that challenge the status quo are often represented as extreme:

It's really bad – women are pushing, it's all extremists . . . I mean women's libbers.

I don't like some people involved in it. Their strong attitudes. They want things that shouldn't be and they want equality.

Lesbians are frequently associated with women's lib and many girls expressed marked prejudice against them:

Have you seen them? Two girls walking along, one of them's got cuff links on and everything, just like a man, I think that's *terrible* – I think it's disgusting.

Poofs I can tolerate but lesbians I can't. I suppose because it's my own sex.

Fear of seduction by lesbian girls was a constant theme – astonishing in the light of the real harassment that girls experience in their day to day life from boys:

Maybe we feel threatened by them – so we think to ourselves 'Oh my god, maybe if they tried to drag me into that thing.'

I think they'd start kind of threatening you, hassling you.

If a close friend came out as a lesbian one girl says:

I wouldn't talk to her as much as I used to, not because I didn't like her as much but because I'd be threatened by her.

Some girls mention TV programmes as influencing their views:

This teacher ... she says we have got to fight against men. It puts you off. Like the Two Ronnies – Life of a Worm – have you seen it? It's like women do everything, men are absolute rubbish. You find a lot of them are lesbians.

Some girls reject the whole idea of women's liberation and were not keen on equal jobs for everyone, reverting to the age-old disinction between the physical strength of men and women:

I don't agree with equal jobs for everyone. Anything mental we can do but physical ... to be honest you wouldn't want to be a truck driver or pull down buildings. Things like furniture removals when you've got to carry heavy loads on your back ... I mean I think there're a lot of things women couldn't do.

Or

I think that women should always be the housewife. I'm not saying she should always cook, but I think, well they [i.e. the roles of men and women] should be a bit joint but I definitely think she should do *most* of it. . . . It wouldn't hurt if the man hoovered though. . . .

Implications

So what contribution can the reform of the education system itself make to encouraging the positive and overcoming the negative aspects of girls' lives in and around the social relations of the school? It is clear that educational reforms should be oriented to the problems of sexual stratification. But the implication is not simply one of extending compensatory education programmes from one area into new ones. Compensatory education has been aimed at male social *mobility*. This is of course viable as regards economic class: assisting working-class kids to become better qualified and get middle-class jobs is at least a coherent strategy. But it makes no sense to apply the concept of 'mobility' to overcoming the effects of sexual stratification: it is a feminist critique which has to be incorporated into the aims of the education system.

Compensatory education programmes have until recently focused exclusively on class. This is in spite of growing recognition of racial and sexual discrimination and inequalities in schools. One difficulty is that teachers who are aware of class

and race differences and disadvantage are much less sympathetic
to equal opportunity policies in regard to girls. At a recent
conference sponsored by the EOC, 'Girl Friendly Schooling'
(1984) the director of a research project reported that the majority
of the teachers surveyed in his research appeared to be in favour
of equal opportunities in principle but were far less committed
in practice. Some teachers claimed that equal opportunities were
irrelevant to their work and some argued that discrimination
was necessary. One said, 'Schools have to prepare pupils for
work in society as it is. Some boys need restricted workspace
more than girls.' A separate paper revealed that secondary
teachers firmly believed that technical education is of greater
importance to boys than to girls. Nearly half the sample thought
that women were not as good as men at complicated technical
problems. 42 per cent thought that a woman's career was not as
important as a man's and 29 per cent that a woman's place was
in the home.[7] One third of the teachers believed that innate
psychological differences between boys and girls were responsible for career choices. So teachers are by no means united in
accepting the need for compensatory programmes for girls or
that equal opportunity programmes are necessary. The question
of how far education can compensate for society is one that
Mary Wollstonecraft posed in the eighteenth century and is still
relevant today:

I don't believe that a private education can work the wonders which
some sanguine writers have attributed to it. Men and women must be
educated, in a great degree, by the opinions and manners of the society
they live in. ... It may ... fairly be inferred that, till society be
differently constituted, much cannot be expected from education
(Wollstonecraft 1792).

Society is not very differently constituted in this respect now but
some progress has been made. But to change education radically
is no easy task. It would involve a curriculum that prepares both
men and women for shared roles in domestic and work life and
stops treating girls as second class citizens, a curriculum that uses
women's experience, knowledge and views of the world. As
Mary Hughes and Mary Kennedy suggest:

It means starting from a different angle and using new hypotheses. It
could be an archaeology class where the concept of gatherer is given

equal importance to that of the hunter; a writing class where the reader's experience is as valid as the author's; a chemistry class which analyses the baking properties of bread; an interior design course which examines the home as a functional place of work, not just as an aesthetic living space; a class on family law which studies the moral and social climate in which the laws were introduced; courses on how films are constructed or the way the film industry works; pre-retirement courses which recognize that women never retire; parent education which emphasises that women and men are parents (Hughes and Kennedy 1985).

As I have shown, even more important than changes in the curriculum are changes in the *social relations* of the school. It is no use changing the curriculum if girls are being harassed and abused and rendered subordinate to boys in the day-to-day interaction of the classroom and the playground. First, the way teachers discriminate against girls needs to be recognized and challenged. The attention that teachers pay to girls needs to be monitored to counteract the tendency to concentrate on boys. Girls must be encouraged to excel in non-traditional subjects. There is still a very low take-up by girls in mixed schools yet in single sex schools girls can achieve better results on average than boys in physics and chemistry. This limits their career opportunities. One way of overcoming this is to run single sex classes in science and maths in mixed schools. Teachers should be aware that boys deprive girls of school facilities, and develop strategies to ensure that this does not occur. Second, the whole question of social relations in schools must be given high a priority. The powerful and taken-for-granted assumptions about sexuality – rather than being natural and biologically given – are social and do not merely reflect but reinforce the subordinate position of girls and women in our society. It is only with a knowledge of how sexual relations are structured by the norms and constraints outlined in this book that progress can be made. This requires a central place for *social* education in the curriculum which is directed at boys as well as girls. The focus of social education should be to prepare both girls and boys for a more egalitarian society.

Unlike sex education in the traditional sense, which usually focuses on different methods of contraception and descriptions of the biological make-up and mechanics of the sex act, social education would focus on the taken-for-granted norms and codes of conduct within which social behaviour takes place. Questions relating to the morality of sexual relations, domestic violence and the objectification of girls would be on the agenda. Instead of focusing purely on the mechanics of contraception, reasons for the fact that only a third of sexually active teenagers actually use contraception would be critically examined (see Spencer 1984). This has been explained by girls' hesitancy about approaching doctors and birth control clinics but what may be more significant is the operation of the double standard that condemns a girl as irresponsible if she does not use contraception, but condemns her as unrespectable if she does use it. It appears that using birth control and contraceptives runs particular risks in relation to a girl's reputation. If she uses contraception on a casual date this involves laying herself open to the charge that sex is premeditated; that she is therefore consciously anticipating that sex might occur with someone she is neither 'in love' nor in a steady relationship with – she is therefore a slag. On the other hand if she has sex without contraception this can be explained by something which 'happens' without previous intent. It is interesting, for example, how often girls describe their sexual encounters not as something that they consciously choose to embark on but as something that 'happens' to them. As Hannah said in an earlier quote:

You might be at a party and someone just dragged you upstairs . . . and the next thing you know you don't know what's happening to you.

Of course, what's happening is rape. But it is too simple to regard the boys as totally blameworthy and 'potential rapists'. They too are locked in to regarding girls in a contradictory way: on the one hand there are pressures on them to regard girls as conquests and to 'make' as many girls as they can; and on the other there are pressures on them as individuals to treat girls well and as friends and to care for them. It is almost as though there are two kinds of sexuality, one that is without emotional feeling and treats women as dirty and provocative, and the other that involves strong feelings of sensuality and compassion; and that these two concepts of sexuality are inextricably linked to the concepts of the virgin and the whore. This may be why the rape of even a virgin or a respectable married woman, as occurred in 'The Rape of Lucretia', is still regarded, if not as the woman's fault, at least as a taint on her character. The boundary between the two types of sexuality has been crossed and the woman, whether it is her fault or not, if raped, has crossed irretrievably into the 'slag' category. This is one reason why so few women report rape to anyone. As we saw in Carol Lee's research (p. 21) on sex education in schools the idea that girls or women provoke rape and are therefore to blame is widespread among adolescents.

It would be easy to counter such notions by pointing out that rape is simply an example of widespread male violence towards women. But the analysis has to go further and question why such views on the nature of rape are so prevalent and uncontested. The girl has to deny her sexual desire to remain respectable, but should she in any way indicate that she is open to advances she is regarded as fair game. The implication then is that rape is not the violent assault that it is in reality but is 'only what women really want'. Now it may be true that women do want to express their sexuality, and do want active sexual lives, but this choice is denied them. Any indication of desire, whether in the form of the way a woman dresses, speaks, looks or flirts is taken as grounds for the man to assault a woman. A slippage has occurred whereby the assumption of desire in a woman turns her from the 'good' virgin into the 'rapacious' whore who will go with anyone anywhere. 'You have to knock them about a bit for them to enjoy it' – and knocked about women are, night after night, month after month, as is shown by the studies of family violence that are emerging out of a wall of silence that has surrounded the cruelty that many women suffer within the privacy of the 'domestic haven'. It is such issues that need to be brought up and questioned in sex education classes, though it is unreasonable to expect teachers to take on such a task without preparation and further training. Rape and violence cannot be explained as the behaviour of psychopathic sex maniacs but rather as actions which are the extension of the normal oppressive structure of sexual relations. It is by challenging the terms on which girls participate in social life that boys and girls can be encouraged to see their relationships not in sexist stereotypical ways or as sex objects, but in terms of their human attributes.

Sex education – in the traditional sense – is also important as there is evidence that girls particularly have little knowledge of their sexual organs and responses, let alone the freedom to express themselves. Jane, in this study, graphically described her sister's fears about her pending wedding:

Jane: She's frightened of the night. She hasn't been to bed with boys or anything so she's frightened. She's getting married this Saturday.

Sandra: Wonder woman she won't be.

Jane: What's she gonna do when he jumps on top of her?

Their description of sex as 'jumping on top of her' and as a scaring experience is hardly a romantic or informed depiction of sexual love.

Tracy, when asked whether anyone talked about sex to her, replied:

My mum does talk about it. When mum explains it she talks like she's carrying a heavy load.

Sexual experience is for many women just like that – carrying a heavy load rather than an experience that lightens their load and lifts them out of themselves.

Likewise, Stevi Jackson in *Learning to Lose* (Spender 1980) describes how the girls she interviewed equated sex with coition and had acquired little information about their own sexual responses or their sexuality. Given the focus on intercourse and reproduction in the knowledge available to adolescents, boys cannot but identify the penis as their chief sexual organ. Most girls, on the other hand, did not even know of the existence of the clitoris. Investigation of the genitals is so heavily tabooed that few girls do so, as is implied by what Sandra and Jane, two girls in this study, say. Third, sexual and racial harassment in schools should be recognized and taken seriously. As Helen put it:

My school work reflects how the rest of my life is going. If I am being sworn at at school or have trouble at home my work suffers.

The sexual abuse that is often a taken-for-granted aspect of everyday life in comprehensive schools amounts to a form of sexual harassment. Sexual harassment and sexual abuse must be taken as seriously as racial abuse. Teachers who turn a blind eye to them or even actively collude in denigrating girls should be disciplined. One difficulty, as I have indicated, is that many

teachers accept the double standard uncritically. A good example of this lack of concern is given by Chris Griffen, who
reported this conversation with a fifth form teacher, Mr Yates,
about girls who reported they had been attacked:

Mr Yates: Some of the girls have been saying they've been attacked
coming to school.

Chris: Yes some did mention that to me.

Mr Yates: Yes, well you don't believe them do you when they say that?

Chris: But if they're worried about it. ...

Mr Yates: Yes, but some of them wouldn't know what it means.
They're just having you on. These attacks are just nothing. They're
not serious you know (Griffen 1985).

Instead of such denial it is time that schools provided self-
defence classes as part of the school curricula.

If some teachers ignore reports of attacks, verbal abuse is even
more likely to be taken for granted or ignored. Yet verbal abuse,
as we have seen, is both denigrating and reinforces the subordination of girls. The use of racist and sexist language is con-
nected to the inferior social roles of blacks and women and
needs to be continually challenged. A disciplinary code should
be drawn up in all schools in which such terms are outlawed and
deemed to be unacceptable. The elimination of sexist language,
as I shall suggest in the final chapter, is a necessary condition for
diminishing sexism in society.

Lastly, a programme to counteract the domestic pressure to abandon work and career requires a revolution in the domestic sphere
as much as in the school. The two as I have stressed earlier in this
chapter are related. It is only when men and women adopt an
equal role in domestic and child care, supported by flexible, state
run child care facilities, that women will be enabled to play an
equal role in society. If everyone worked around twenty hours a
week this would both eliminate unemployment and enable men
and women to lead more balanced and fulfilling lives.

Notes

1   Quoted by Deirdre Beddoe, *Discovering Women's History*,
1983, p. 61.

2   In the first ten years of the act not one complaint of educational discrimination has been upheld. See Weiner, Gaby, *Just a Bunch of Girls*, Open University, 1985, p. 2.
3   See also the discussion by M. MacDonald in 'Schooling and the Reproduction of Class and Gender Relations', in L. Barton *et al.*, *Schooling, Ideology and the Curriculum*, Falmer Press, 1980, pp. 28–47.
4   One major reason is that few apprenticeship schemes are open to girls.
5   See Mary Fuller's description (1980) of West Indian girls who conformed to the notion of 'good pupil' by working hard but who behaved badly in class and were anti school. Being pro-learning and pro-school did not go together.
6   According to two surveys carried out in 1971 and 1981 by Peter Bunhill and Andrew McPherson, women in 1981 were more likely than in 1971 to have well formed views about what they wanted from an 'ideal job'. 'Careers and gender: the expectations of able Scottish school leavers in 1971 and 1981', in Sandra Acker and David Piper (eds), *Is Higher Education Fair to Women?*, SHRE and NFER-NELSON, 1984.
7   Margaret Spear's study was based on samples of secondary school teachers in mixed comprehensives in southern England (Institute of Educational Technology, Open University).

Bibliography

Allport, G., *The Nature of Prejudice*, Addison Wesley, 1954.
Arnot, M., 'How shall we educate our sons?', in R. Deem (ed.), *Coeducation Reconsidered*, Open University Press, 1984.
Beddoe, D., *Discovering Women's History*, Pandora Press, 1983.
Delamont, S., *Sex Roles and the School*, Methuen, 1980.
EOC, *Girl Friendly Schooling*, 1984.
Fogelman, K., *Britain's Sixteen Year Olds*, National Children's Bureau, 1976.
Fuller, H., 'Black Girls in a London Comprehensive School', in Deem, R., *Schooling for Women's Work*, Routledge and Kegan Paul, 1980.
Griffen, Chris, *Typical Girls*, Routledge and Kegan Paul, 1985.
Holt, J., *How Children Fail*, Pelican, 1964.
Hooks, Bell, *Ain't I a Woman*, South End Press, Boston, 1981.
Hughes, Mary and Kennedy, Mary, *New Futures: Changing Women's Education*, Routledge and Kegan Paul, 1985.

King, L., 'Unequal access in education – sex and social class', *Social Administration*, **5** no. 3 (1981), pp. 167–75.

Lerner, Gerda, *Black Women in White America*, quoted in Bell Hooks 1981.

Llewellyn, M., 'Studying Girls at School: the implications of confusion', in Deem, R. (ed.), *Schooling for Women's Work*, Routledge and Kegan Paul, 1980.

MacDonald, M., 'Schooling and the Reproduction of Class and Gender Relations', in L. Barton *et al.*, *Schooling, Ideology and the Curriculum*, Falmer Press, 1980.

Marks, P., 'Femininity in the Classroom', in Mitchell, J. and Oakley, A., *The Rights and Wrongs of Women*, Pelican, 1976.

Marshall, J., 'Developing Anti-Sexist Education', *International Journal of Political Education*, **16** no. 2 (1983).

McRobbie, A., 'Working class girls and the culture of femininity', in *Women Take Issue*, Women's Study Group, Anchor Press, 1978.

Payne, I., 'A Working Class Girl in a Grammar School', in Spender D. and Sarah, E. (eds.), *Learning to Lose*, Women's Press, 1980.

Spencer, B., 'Young men: their attitudes towards sexuality and birth control', *British Journal of Family Planning*, **10** 1984, pp. 13–19.

Spender, D. and Sarah, E. (eds.), *Learning to Lose*, Womens Press, 1980.

Spender, D., *Invisible Women*, Writers and Readers Press, 1982.

Toynbee, P., Article in *Guardian*, 21 March 1983.

Willis, P., *Learning to Labour*, Saxon House, 1977.

5 Language and discourse

'But "glory" doesn't mean "a nice knock-down argument,"' Alice objected.

'When *I* use a word,' Humpty Dumpty said in a rather scornful tone, 'it means just what I choose it to mean – neither more nor less.'

'The question is,' said Alice, 'whether you *can* make words mean different things.'

'The question is,' said Humpty Dumpty, 'which is to be master – that's all.' (Lewis Carroll, *Through the Looking-Glass*)

On setting out to explore the lives of adolescent girls as portrayed through their own accounts of their experiences, one further inadequacy of previous research into female adolescence stands out. This is the view that adolescence is the age of turbulence when adult values are challenged and rejected and problems such as delinquency, drug addiction, sexual promiscuity, and hooliganism are rampant; and all's well that ends well when young men (girls are rarely mentioned) settle down to the respectability of married life. On one level these assumptions about adolescence are right – delinquency, drug addiction and violence are greater then than later. Yet what characterizes the behaviour of most teenagers far more than their turbulence is their conformity, conformity to a patriarchal sexist society in which both sexes lose out. The boys, who are prepared like boxers for a fight to earn their living, find a wife to provide them with a family, yet retain their sexual and social freedom; the girls, even today, are prepared for a life centred on domesticity and motherhood, any career aspirations or personal ambition or freedom holding second place to the ideal of finding the man of their dreams. The realization that this dream of suburban bliss is no longer realizable with unemployment rising and women challenging their inequality has only just begun to percolate down to modify these ideals. Like Willis, I was interested in adolescence not as a period of turbulence – the girls I interviewed described few disagreements with their parents and particularly close relationships with their mothers – but as a process of conformity and transition into adult life. In particular I was interested in how girls become wives and mothers.

In tune with much recent feminist research I wanted to explore the way girls themselves saw their lives *in their own terms* rather than ask preconceived, structured questions. This method requires a qualitative in-depth approach to interviewing so that the individual's way of conceptualizing her experience can be followed up. One difficulty that arises is that language is inadequate for describing women's experience. This emerges in two ways. First, language depicts girls in terms of their marital status or sexual activity. We have seen, for example, how few words of sexual abuse apply to men and how there is no vocabulary to describe the actively sexual woman – apart from derogatory abuse. Dale Spender in *Man Made Language* reports a study by Julia Stanley[1] of words used to describe women and found that far more of these referred to sexual behaviour than was the case for men. 220 words referred to a sexually promiscuous female and only twenty to a sexually promiscuous male. Sexual behaviour on the part of men, however, is aggressively active. As Germaine Greer puts it: 'All the vulgar linguistic emphasis is placed on the poking element – fucking, screwing, rooting, shagging – are all acts performed upon the passive female. The names for the penis are all tool names.'

Woman is not primarily defined in terms of her humanity but in terms of her marital or sexual status – wife, mother or spinster – or in terms of feminine or sexual categories – as virgin or whore. Second, and linked to this secondary status in language, women are often deputed as the *object* of male experience or do not acquire what Maria Black and Rosalind Coward call non-gendered subjectivity. They describe the way a masculine model is implicit in language in this way:

Men remain men and women become specific categories in relation to men and to other categories. Prince Charles and Lady Diana Spencer disappeared into the church and emerged as man and wife. Being a man is an entitlement not to masculine attributes but to non-gendered subjectivity.

It is this non-gendered subjectivity that women never really have. Women normally adopt their husband's names on marriage and are invariably known not merely as Mrs but often as the wife of their husband's occupation – doctor's wife, vicar's wife and so on. In *Small Changes* Marge Piercy describes how difficult it is to find a woman friend if you do not know her married name. 'She had to find out that strange name before she could find her – Miriam Berry was no more. Abolished. Women must often lose a friend that way and never be able to find each other again.' (Piercy 1973).

Language is deficient in words describing women's active experience. Betty Friedan has a phrase for a housewife's lot: 'the problem that has no name'. This describes the dissatisfaction and depression that women feel stuck in the home all day (Friedan 1976). The aim of this research was therefore always to take the girls' own descriptions and raise questions about the way they describe their lives, their experiences, their relationships and their aspirations for the future. Two important questions arise from these descriptions. First, how does the language of sexual abuse structure their experiences, and second, can this language of abuse be challenged? In this chapter I shall take up these two questions within the context of current feminist debate.

The first question I wish to raise is how to make sense of experience. A focus on experience does not imply a dismissal of theory in the way some feminist researchers have suggested. Nor can a simple distinction between rationality and experience be upheld. It is not a question of choosing experience over rationality. Stanley and Wise (1983) for example, argue that experience is superior to rationality, failing to appreciate that our experience of the world involves a cognitive process of making sense of perceptions and emotions through a process of labelling which involves categorization and conceptualization. There is no such thing as what they call 'raw experience': experience is always socially constructed. Individuals who create social relationships are, as I suggested in the introduction, themselves social creations. As Hartsock (1979) argues, to develop an understanding of the world it is vital to examine the very categories with which we handle and experience it:

We must understand that theorizing is not just something done by academic intellectuals but that a theory is always implicit in our activity

and goes so deep as to include our very understanding of reality
... we can either accept the categories given to us by capitalist society
or we can begin to develop a critical understanding of our world. If we
choose the first alternative our theory may forever remain implicit.
In contrast, the second is to commit ourselves to working out critical
and explicit theory (Hartsock 1979).

It is not enough to take experience at face value but we need to
examine the implicit assumptions that underlie the constraints,
in this case, on girls' lives. To argue that experience is superior
to theory is to accept experience uncritically without taking into
consideration how it is itself a product of unfair relations
between the sexes. It is to fail to take into account that the way
we understand the world is a product of theoretical assumptions
that need to be made explicit and understood. By analysing what
girls say it becomes clear that what they say has a shared though
hidden organization that structures, indeed produces, those cultural meanings through which they relate to the world. We too
have been fashioned by the same culture and, however critical
we may be of such categories as 'slag' and 'tight bitch', we are
subject to their objectification and our sexuality is constrained by
their power. It is here that our experience as women becomes
important in carrying out the research. The research technique
focused on reading the transcriptions of the interviews and
group discussions as text rather than as the source of facts. In
focusing on the meanings/explanations as presented, in order to
make sense of what the girls said, we looked at what the accounts
have in common in terms of explanations, contradictions, oppo-
sitions, gaps and taken-for-granted assumptions (see Appendix
for Content Analysis Schedule). The aim was always to make
explicit the hidden or unexpressed assumptions behind the explanations given. The realization for example that slag, rather
than necessarily relating to actual sexual behaviour, relates to
whether the girl labelled is unattached or appears to be unattached, only emerged from studying the way slag is actually
used and not used; we did not focus on the girls' own awareness
of how the term is used.

Discourse analysis

This method resembles what has come to be termed discourse
analysis, which is a particular way of analysing how ideas,

or ideology, function as a system of power and domination. Derived from the work of Foucault (1979), the method tries to get away from the reductionism of more traditional marxist approaches to the study of ideology. Marion Black and Rosalind Coward describe the issue in this way:

Language and the meanings produced therein are not expressive of any simple social division be it class, sex or whatever. If we do not want to reduce language to a simple instrument or effect of a class or sex position but to see it as something productive of the positions we can occupy, then we have to ... see discourses as determinate forms of social practice with their own conditions of existence in other social practices (e.g. political, economic, or scientific) and in social relations and as having definite effects, with regard to those practices and relations ... it is *to insist that language has a material existence* [my italics]. It defines our possibilities and limitations, it constitutes our subjectivities (Black and Coward 1981).

This is exactly the approach I have tried to take in this book. Unlike more traditional and marxist theories of ideology I have not tried to see the language of 'slag' as the *reflection* or form of *appearance* – a surface froth of real relations of male control over women that underlie it. This is the more traditional marxist approach. There is no 'base' or 'material substratum' of which the language of slags and drags is the verbal and mental reflection of the 'superstructure'. All sorts of people are continually engaging in practices through which the language is used and perpetuated: parents urging particular courses of action on their daughters with regard to career and marriage, mothers evaluating the relative importance of homework versus housework as far as their daughters are concerned, teachers talking to girls and boys in different ways and emphasizing different aspects of the curriculum, boys chiding girls who try to be active and show their own initiative, girls labelling those who show such independence as 'show-offs'. There is no hidden reality of power of which all these things are the appearance. Rather they *are* the material practices, the discourses of sexist power and the myriad of conversations and actions which daily constitute it. Being called a slag, redeeming oneself in certain ways (getting a steady boyfriend), discussing whether one's friends are slags, blaming the girl for precipitating rape, for putting up with sexual violence – this is the practice of the language of sexual power, not a reflection of some other process hidden from view. The actions and evaluations and labelling of one another by girls and of girls by boys is the operation of a particular *discourse* about sexuality and moral worth. The language of slag is not exercised by boys over girls, rather both sexes inhabit a world structured by the language quite irrespective of who speaks to or about whom. The double standard of morality is so embedded in language and in the conceptions of masculinity and femininity that girls rarely contest them. Likewise, the discourse of slag plays a crucial role in the constitution of male relationships. As Cynthia Cockburn describes in her account of male compositors,

Many women who have had reason to work with compositors will confirm my experience that they make a big show of apologizing for 'bad language' that would offend a woman's ears. By this they don't mean the odd 'damn' or 'bloody'. The social currency of the compositing room is woman and women objectifying talk, from sexual expletives and innuendo through to narration of exploits or fantasies. The wall is graced with four colour litho 'tits' and 'bums'. Even the computer is used to produce life size print outs of naked women (Cockburn 1983).

A useful way to understand how terms like slag are used is provided by Colin Sumner in a study of the functioning of *categories of deviance*:

Their general function is to denounce and control not to explain. . . . They mark off the deviant, the pathological, the dangerous and the criminal from the normal and the good . . . [they] are not just labels . . . [but] . . . . They are loaded with implied interpretations of real phenomena, models of human nature and the weight of political self interest (Sumner 1983).

To call a girl a slag is to use a term that, as we have seen, appears at first sight to be a label describing an actual form of behaviour but one into which no girl incontrovertibly fits. It is even difficult to identify what actual behaviour is specified. Take Helen's description of how appearance can define girls, not in terms of their attributes as human beings, but in terms of sexual reputation:

I mean they might not mean any harm. I mean they might not be as bad as they look. But their appearance makes them stand out and that's what makes them look weird and you think 'God I can imagine her y'know?' .... She straight way gets a bad reputation even though the girl might be decent inside. She might be good. She might still be living at home. She might just want to look different but might still act normal.

You cannot imagine a boy's appearance being described in this way. How she dresses determines how a girl is viewed and how she is viewed is in terms of her assumed sexual behaviour. Whether or not she is 'good' or not is determined by how she is assumed to conduct her sexual life, that sexuality being relative to male sexual needs.

Rather than attempt to specify what particular behaviour differentiates a slag it is more useful to see slag as what Sumner terms a category of 'moral censure': as part of a discourse about behaviour as a departure, or potential departure from – in this case – male conceptions of female sexuality which run deep in the culture, so deep that the majority of men and women cannot formulate them except by reference to these terms of censure that signal a threatened violation. This violation can occur for no reason other than a rebuff from a girl, as we saw in the first chapter:

What I hate is when a boy tries, you go somewhere and a boy tries to sort of get in with you and if you dislike him as a person, then [he says] 'Slag'. That's what really annoys me.

A girl should be flattered by a boy's interest, should be a passive and compliant recipient rather than an active agent in her own right. She can be deemed a slag both when she approaches him or rebuffs him. He must always be master.

The other facet of the way slag operates is in its uncontested status as a category. Girls, when faced with sexual abuse, react by denying the accusation rather than by objecting to the use of the category. For them, what is important is to prove that you are not a slag. Even when the boy does not know her, the girl reacts by focusing on the injustice of the application of the abuse rather than the use of the category itself:

I've been walking down the street and someone's said to me, across the road, being rude, and says '*You slag*' and I think 'How do you know? *You've got no evidence.*' That makes me angry 'cos like you see someone and you're meant to know whether they sleep around or not.

The girl is concerned with how the term applied to her – what she unquestionably accepts is the legitimacy of the category of slag.

In another interview Wendy, asked what she would do if someone called her a slag, replies:

I'd turn round and say *'Why? Tell me why.'* And then if they said because you were with so and so last week, then if I'd liked them I'd just say, You knew I liked them. I was just unlucky enough for them to chuck me. It's not my fault. It just happened. It's not as though I did it just for sex, just because I wanted someone to sleep with that night.

Here Wendy is assuming she actually has slept with a boy and she justifies her action by arguing that she liked the boy and that it just 'happened'. What she fails to do is to take up the iniquity of the boy's accusation. When accusations do not even relate to actual sexual behaviour, rather than rejecting the abuse, the problem then becomes one of proving your 'innocence'. The problem for the other girls is to find out whether the accusations are true or not.

What is lacking is a language through which the legitimacy of slag as a way of censoring girls can be contested. This is analogous to recognizing and contesting sexual harassment, which was until recently regarded as something women enjoyed. Sexist abuse is, however, so much taken for granted that it is rarely contested in the way that racist abuse is. The power relations underlying such abuse are rarely recognized and any tendency to rebel or hit out against the effects of sexual subordination is seen by men – and other women too – as unwarranted behaviour. One of the girls in this study describes behaviour that she regards as showing off:

One of these girls was walking down the road near the school and somebody whistled to her, a man, and she turned round and waved. If that had been me I would've just looked down and pretended it didn't happen. Even if there was nobody around I don't think you should turn around and wave, would you? It makes you think badly of them don't it. You think what kind of a home have they been brought up in? If I'd done that my dad would've given me a wallop I would never forget. I wouldn't do it anyway.

Q   What do you think it means?

Giving him the 'come on' signs.

The chauvinism of boys on the other hand, though noticed, goes uncontested and is accepted as 'what boys are like':

Mina: As soon as he's got that (sex) from you he's off, just saying 'had my piece from her'. Off he goes and news travels around. Some boys like to boast about it.

When girls do complain about the sexism of boys this opens them up to further attacks. Take this example from Pat Mahony's girls:

We were walking along talking when a couple of boys aged about fourteen began edging towards us. One passed unnecessarily close and growled to his mate: 'Cor I'd like to squeeze her tits'. Amazed, we turned to the boy and told him how disgusting his attitude was. 'How dare we speak to him like that . . . obviously slags, slags, slags, slags'. . . . He continued to shout loudly at us as we continued out of the school (Mahony 1985).

Girls make distinctions between boys and suspect there are not many boys you can trust. Yet they rarely appear to attack the sexism nor question the morality of the boy's behaviour. It is natural for a boy to behave in a downright egotistical, dishonest, bolshy, untrustworthy, unfeeling way. They are plugged into defending their reputation with all the odds against them.

What characterizes the way slag functions as a term of moral censure is on the one hand its uncontested nature as a category, and on the other hand its elusiveness and denigratory force. In this book I have illustrated how discourses operate in a number of areas of the girls' lives, regarding in particular sexuality, friendships and marriage.

Sexuality

The language of 'slag' forms part of a discourse on sexuality which is overwhelmingly characterized by a double standard. It is seen as natural for boys to be after one thing in their relationships with girls – sex. A boy gains kudos from openly boasting of his sexual exploits and in particular a reputation for promiscuity gains a boy respect. And, after all, sex is giving a girl what she really wants. By contrast for a girl to initiate sex is seen as wrong and a slur on her reputation – she becomes a slag. Similarly if a girl engages in premeditated sex by taking contraceptive precautions. To want sex at all for a girl is to become an object of disdain. This double standard lies behind the dilemma faced by girls of slag or drag, virgin or whore. To initiate sex is unfeminine behaviour, yet at the same time girls are seen as responsible for boys' sexual urges. Girls 'ask for it' and a girl has only herself to blame ultimately if an encounter with a boy results in rape. This contradiction between sexual awareness as 'dirty' and at the same time being responsible for leading boys on lies behind the division of girls into the two categories, reproduced through the centuries, of virgin and whore.

There is a second, closely related, element of this double standard. While for boys an active sex life enhances personal reputation, boys are not judged simply in terms of their sexual activity. They have access to that world of 'non-gendered subjectivity' of sport, work, academic achievement which for a girl is always secondary to her sexual reputation. All her behaviour has a sexual significance whatever she is trying to do or achieve. And as I have tried to show, this is a reflection of adult social life in general. The ultimate consequence of this discourse is the control over girls to the advantage of boys, a form of control which steers girls into 'acceptable' forms of sexuality and social behaviour.

Friendships

Closely allied to the discourse on sexuality is that on friendship. Precisely because all girls' behaviour has sexual significance then it follows that they are seen as incapable of the type of true friendship and comradeship which exists among boys. Girls are said to compete for male attention and see other girls as rivals. This discourse clouds the reality that girls must attach themselves to boys and boys' interests to gain access to the public world. Boys' social and recreational activities define the social world in which girls move. It is legitimate for boys to ignore their girlfriends and spend all night in the pub talking to their mates and indeed to talk about girls in sexist ways in front of them. Boys can be bitchy to girls but this is just 'acting big'. If boys engage in sexual harassment of girls or even physical violence, then one way or another it is the girls' ultimate fault either for initiating it in the first place through some form of social provocation or for putting up with it when it does take place or both. Violence and aggression from boys are legitimised in a variety of ways. Boys 'don't really mean it' or are 'just taking out their anger' or perhaps they have been provoked beyond endurance (by a girl of course) or, even, the girl 'really' likes the odd slap from her boyfriend.

Marriage

An important theme in my argument has been that the discourse on marriage is largely negative. Marriage is seen as inevitable and once you get married you 'lose pride in yourself'. Most men won't lift a finger around the house, wives are tied to the home with little freedom, often deprived of money, doing menial wage labour on top of domestic chores and expected to be there at their husband's beck and call. But the girls do get married and regard it as a natural event. I tried to suggest some of the ways in which they reconciled themselves to something spoken of so negatively and it is here of course that the power of the discourse on sexuality reveals itself – as steering the girls towards a married existence as the only legitimate form of sexuality.

As important as what the discourse includes is what it excludes. Nowhere is the loss of a woman's identity implicit in taking the man's name focused upon. Similar silences surround the economic dependency of wives on husbands and the restriction that marriage places on the career opportunities of women – their access to the non-gendered subjectivity of the male public world. Finally, until very recently, discourse on marriage was silent on the extent of violence by husbands against wives and children. Even today, the imprecise term 'domestic violence' clouds the reality: *male* violence against *women*. Falling in love which, as we have seen, is the only legitimate way for girls to express sexual desire, is also the only legitimate basis for marriage. Romantic love with its connotation of a relationship between equals becomes, in marriage, a relationship between unequals. Thus the inequalities in marriage as an institution are obscured. On the contrary, it is men who are said to be 'trapped' into marriage. It is therefore at the level of discourse that we should locate the oppression of women. This view contrasts with attempts to explain the oppression of women in modern society by their confinement to the private sphere.

There are problems with reducing woman's subordination to either her role in the family (the private sphere) or in the labour market and public life (the public sphere). First, why are women in an inferior position in the private sphere? It is one thing to find economic or other reasons why women spend the bulk of their lives in the private domain, but this does not, of itself, explain why their position in that sphere should be one of subordination to men (see Harris (1981) on Delphy). Equally, to show that the roles and activities of the private sphere are predominantly organized around reproduction and child care is not to explain why men exercise control over women. Such domination cannot be explained simply by reference to men's greater freedom to participate in the public sphere and hence their absence from the private. For why should absence lead to domination? Anthropologists such as Harris (1981) and Rosaldo (1980) cite many examples of cultures in which male supremacy is retained despite considerable, and at times equal, participation of women and men in public life.

Second, explanations that separate the public and private spheres often amount to tautologies. *Whatever* women do – and their roles vary between societies and through time – tends to become assimilated to the category of 'domestic' labour. Various types of work such as making tea, cleaning up, typing etc., tend to be characterized as 'women's work' whether they are done at home or in the office or works canteen.

Discourse analysis as used in this book attempts to overcome these problems by focusing on the language of sexuality as a form of activity or material practice in itself – rather than an ideological reflection of other practices – discourse analysis is in a position to grasp the dynamics of female subordination to men not in terms of, but rather irrespective of, the separation between the public and the private spheres. The language of sexual discourse, the activity of describing, naming and labelling goes on equally in both spheres.

Thus following Foucault (1980) the discussion of power does not relate to whether girls are concentrated in certain roles rather than others but can be seen as a field of force in which boys and girls are equally trapped rather than being exercised by boys over girls. Thus it is less important to show, as Pat Mahony vividly portrays, that boys use a different language to abuse others than girls do (Mahony 1985) than to realize that whoever is talking, virtually all of the terms of abuse available are ones which denigrate women.

What this research suggests, then, is that although for girls to sleep with a steady boyfriend before marriage is certainly more common than thirty years ago, the double standard of sexual morality is just as strong today. Public debates about adolescent girls however focus not on girls' inequality with boys but rather on their assumed promiscuity and drop in moral standards. Changes such as the increase in the use of contraception have occurred, yet the central mythology of sex gender relations lives on.

Conclusion:
can sexual abuse be challenged?

The analysis of sexist language discourses epitomizing the oppression of women is crucially relevant to how change can occur. The argument that language will change only if behaviour changes is dubious. Robin Lakoff for example argues that only if society changes:

> so that the distinction between married and unmarried women is as unimportant in terms of their social position as that between married and unmarried men will 'Ms' have a chance of gaining general acceptance (Lakoff 1975).

But the two cannot be separated in principle. Though there is obviously a difference between talking about something and doing it, this is not the point since both are examples of human action. The argument that if men and women were treated equally then sexist terminology would fall into disuse is simply asserting that if we change one form of behaviour then others will change as a consequence. It could just as plausibly be argued that unless we first get rid of sexist terminology it will not be possible to treat people equally. The chicken and egg argument is pointless. What we have to do is change human action of which speech is one component. The change in sexist language is not something that will follow on from changes in the real mechanisms of power. Rather, changing the language of sexism *is* changing the practices of power. As Thorne and Henley argue in opposition to Robin Lakoff:

> To call people Mrs or Miss is to help maintain a definition of woman which relegates them primarily to family roles. To use he or she rather than he for sex indefinite antecedents is a tangible gesture for including rather than excluding women from consciousness. Males who consistently interrupt females in conversation are engaging in acts of social dominance. In short, verbal and non-verbal communication

patterns are not simply epiphenomena, they help to establish, transmit and maintain male dominance. Language change is obviously not the whole story, but it is certainly part of social change (Thorne and Henley 1975).

Nor is it the case that language change is impossible. Dale Spender asserts in her book *Man Made Language* that it is a semantic contradiction (i.e. not possible in the English Language) to formulate representations of women's autonomy and strength. However as Maria Black and Rosalind Coward point out, Spender confuses characteristics of the grammatical structure of language with the particular discourses conducted within it:

The issue is how did certain idioms and stereotypical phrases like *men and women* arise and why are idioms often a central component of discourses where they function *as if* they were required by the structure of language, the organization of society or 'human nature' (Black and Coward 1981).

It is obviously not the case that phrases such as 'in no woman's land' or 'a person should stand on her own two feet' are semantically impossible otherwise I could not just have said them. But it is true that every day speech reproduces a window on the world and on sexuality from the standpoint of men and it will go on reproducing such a standpoint *because it is not opposed*: and this is a political rather than an epistemological question.[1]

What needs to be done is to challenge the discourses and the social relations of 'moral censure' which they embody. Whether such a challenge can succeed is a question of forces and mobilization. But one consequence of the resurgence of the feminist movement is precisely the development of such a practice. Change has not been negligible even though it has gone further in the United States than in Britain where the leader of the EOC is still referred to as chairman. As Wendy Martyna says, with reference to the United States:

Language change may be difficult, but it is not impossible. Some prominent individuals for example, have made striking changes in their language use ... a variety of government agencies, feminist groups, professional associations, religious organizations, educational institutions have also endorsed language change, issuing guidelines or passing regulations concerning sexist language. Initially empirical studies suggest considerable language changes among university faculty and politicians.

Terms such as 'chairman' and Miss and Mrs must be challenged if women are to gain recognition as human beings on equal terms to men. Sexual graffiti and abuse must be outlawed – the recent walk out by teachers from Poundswick High School in Manchester when ordered to take back pupils who had written obscene graffiti about some of them and their wives, is a welcome development and a sign that teachers are beginning to take action.

To change the language of sexuality will be difficult as it challenges our basic assumptions about masculinity and femininity. Yet the language of sexuality must change if women are to be sexually liberated. As Susan Sontag points out:

Merely to remove the onus placed upon the sexual expressiveness of women is a hollow victory if the sexuality they become freer to enjoy remains the old one that converts women into objects. ... This already 'freer' sexuality mostly reflects a spurious idea of freedom: the right of each person briefly to exploit and dehumanize someone else. Without a change in the very norms of sexuality the liberation of women is a meaningless goal. Sex as such is not liberating for women. Neither is more sex (quoted in N. Keohane, M. Rosaldo and B. Gelpi (eds.), *Feminist Theory: A Critique of Ideology*, Harvester Press, 1982, p. 19).

What is needed is a revolution in the way language is used. The pessimistic picture painted in this research implies that despite the gains women have made over the last century – achieving the vote and greater legal rights, improved access to education, contraception and abortion, and more economic and social freedom, the language of sexuality has hardly changed. The discourses relating to sexuality and women's inferior position in marriage and society – have not altered. They continue to act coercively to deprive women of non-gendered subjectivity – to consideration as human beings rather than sexual objects. The sexual insults that we have seen to be part and parcel of every day interaction in school, are oppressive and denigrating and embrace a hatred of women and a desire to dominate and oppress. Inequality within marriage is legitimized by such discourses and even violence is condoned in the domestic sphere or rarely taken seriously and both the police and social agencies tend to regard it as a private matter.[2] Some pornography does not just symbolize women's subordination, but is part of the active process of maintaining that subordination. In just the same way, the language of sexual abuse is part of the coercive process of social control which ultimately prevents the liberation of women.

Notes

1 Some structuralists tend to regard discourses as such an all determining constitutive process that any critique of change seems almost out of the question – though somehow miraculously the theorist who is pointing all this out is exempted from the grip of the discourse. As Bob Connell has pointed out:

The 'reproduction of social relations' is a chimera. In all structures it never occurs; it cannot occur. We cannot treat social structure as something persisting in its identity behind the backs of mortal people, who are inserted into their places by a cosmic cannery called reproduction. ... Rather we have to shift standpoint. The continuity, the persistence through time, with which theory is concerned does not have the ontological structure of a reproduced identity, but that of an intelligible succession. It is not a relation of similarity between the structure today and the structure yesterday that is the point but a relation of practice between them, the way one was produced out of the other (Connell 1983).

'Reproduction' is simply the absence of a practice challenging what has gone before. The point as Connell emphasizes is to discover how certain practices are challenged and thereby changed.
2 See Kathryn McCann's article 'Battered Women and the Law', in J. Brophy and C. Smart (eds.), *Women in Law*, Routledge and Kegan Paul, 1985.

Bibliography

Black, M. and Coward, R., 'Linguistic, Social and Sexual Relations', *Screen Education*, **39** (1981).
Cockburn, C., *Brothers. Male Dominance and Technological Change*, Pluto, 1983.

Connell, R. W., *Which Way is Up? Essays on Class, Sex and Culture*, Allen & Unwin, 1983.

Friedan, B., *The Feminine Mystique*, Penguin, 1976.

Foucault, M., *The History of Sexuality*, vol. 1, Allen Lane, 1979.

Harris, O., 'Households as natural units', in *Of Marriage and the Market*, K. Young, C. Wolkowitz and R. McCullagh (eds.), CSE Books, 1981.

Hartsock, N., *Feminist Theory and Revolutionary Strategy in Capitalist Patriarchy and the Case for Socialist Feminism*, Monthly Review Press, 1979.

Lakoff, Robin, *Language and Woman's Place*. Harper and Row, 1975.

Mahony, P., *Schools for the Boys?*, Hutchinson, 1985.

Martyna, Wendy, 'Beyond the "He/Man" Approach: the Case for Nonsexist Language', *Signs*, **5**, no. 3 (Spring 1980).

Piercy, M., *Small Changes*, Fawcett Crest, 1973.

Rosaldo, M., 'The Use and Abuse of Anthropology: Reflections on Feminism and Cross Cultural Understanding', *Signs*, **5**, no. 3 (1980).

Spender, D., *Man Made Language*, Routledge and Kegan Paul, 1980.

Stanley, L. and Wise, S., *Breaking Out. Feminist Consciousness and Feminist Research*, Routledge and Kegan Paul, 1983.

Sumner, C., 'Rethinking Deviance Towards a Sociology of Censures', *Research in Law, Deviance and Social Control*, vol. 5, JAI Press, 1983.

Thorne, Barry and Henley, Nancy (eds.), *Language and Sex*, Newbury House, 1975.

Appendix

The attached schedule was drawn up and each transcribed interview and discussion was read carefully and then cut up and sorted into the categories. It was then possible to compare what different girls said about each category and examine the terms in which they described their experiences.

Content analysis schedule

Contents

1   Friends
1.1   Sharing/understanding
1.2   Trust/confide
1.3   Activities with friends
1.4   Talking with friends
1.5   Forming friends/changing friends/dropping friends for boys
1.6   Agreeing/being similar
1.7   Friends help you
1.8   General picture of friends class/girls
1.9   What makes a girl popular with other girls
1.10 Without friends (interests without friends)

2   Talk
2.1   Talk about other girls
2.2   Talk about boys
2.3   Talk about clothes
2.4   Talk about problems
2.5   Talk about sex
2.6   Talk about school
2.7   Talk about what happened last night/what is going to happen

2.8   Talk about pop stars
2.9   Talking behind your back
2.10 Talk about politics

3   Bitchiness
3.1   Girls are bitchy or not
3.2   Bitchiness about clothes
3.3   Bitchiness about boys
3.4   Bitchiness as jealousy
3.5   Bitchiness about superiority/inferiority
3.6   Bragging

4   Boys
4.1   Fancying boys
4.2   Attractive boys/Flirts
4.3   Nice boys
4.4   Boys treat you bad
4.5   How boys talk about girls
4.6   Boys together
4.7   Avoid boys/not go out much
4.8   Why go out with boys/expectations/talk
4.9   Boyfriends
4.10 What makes a girl popular with boys
4.11 Getting on with boys (in general)
4.12 Dropping girlfriends

5   Girls you don't like
5.1   Bullies
5.2   Flash girls/smart
5.3   Sluttish girls
5.4   Posh girls/Trendy girls/Lesbians
5.5   Lower class girls
5.6   Achievers at school
5.7   Girls distrust each other – girls are bitchy
5.8   Dishonest girls

6   Having fun
6.1   Friends make you laugh
6.2   Sharing jokes
6.3   Making fun of others
6.4   Teasing/bullying others for fun

6.5 Doing silly things for fun
6.6 Making fun of teachers
6.7 What sort of things are funny
6.8 Jokes and teachers

7 Sexuality and slag
7.1 Slag as name-calling/bitchiness/to start an argument
7.2 Talking to boys gets you a name
7.3 Slag as jealousy for looks/clothes/being popular with boys
7.4 Sleeping around
7.5 Double standard
7.6 Slag as dirty/not decent
7.7 How to get to be respectable again/how to counteract 'slag'
7.8 Sex before marriage or not
7.9 Is reputation catching/are girls dropped if labelled 'slag'?
7.10 Slag and class

8 Arguments/violence/fights
8.1 Trouble over boys/jealousy/girls
8.2 Arguments between friends
8.3 Violence in school
8.4 Violence in the street/club etc
8.5 The Fight and other fights

9 School
9.1 Bunking off school
9.2 Hating school/not liking school
9.3 Liking school
9.4 Good teachers
9.5 Bad teachers
9.6 Injustice
9.7 Mucking-about
9.8 If you can't understand the work
9.9 Homework
9.10 Class differences in school
9.11 Girls teachers like/don't like
9.12 Mixed schools versus single sex

10 The future
10.1 In general
10.2a Careers

Index